The Revolt of the Palestinian Jews

The Revolt

of the
Palestinian Jews

How the Netanyahu Government
Invited the October 7 Massacre

ANTHONY CARDINALE

RESOURCE *Publications* · Eugene, Oregon

Resource Publications
An Imprint of Wipf and Stock Publishers
199 W. 8th Ave., Suite 3
Eugene, OR 97401

www.wipfandstock.com

PAPERBACK ISBN: 979-8-3852-2256-8
HARDCOVER ISBN: 979-8-3852-2257-5
EBOOK ISBN: 979-8-3852-2258-2

VERSION NUMBER 06/24/24

For Steve Lipman

"Enough already about the poor Palestinian Arabs—
what about the Palestinian Jews who were there first?"

—REMARK OVERHEARD IN A SYNAGOGUE

"Love the stranger, for you were strangers in the land of Egypt."

—DEUT 10:19 (one of 36 references to this command in the Pentateuch)

The world will never forgive Israel for allegedly committing genocide
in Gaza. Is it possible that, someday, the Palestinian Arab casualties
in Israel's war against Hamas will become the excuse for the nations to
attack Israel in the end times, as prophesied in the Bible?

Contents

ALSO BY ANTHONY CARDINALE

The Red Heifer: A Jewish Cry for Messiah

> "*The Red Heifer* is an extraordinary piece of literature,
> well researched, and extremely timely. I found it to be
> well worth reading and I highly recommend it!"
> —Rabbi Michael Wolf, Congregation Beth Messiah,
> Cincinnati

The Pharisees Are Coming to Jesus: Secret Orthodox Believers in Israel and America

> "Cardinale has taken a controversial topic that melds
> Christianity with Judaism and deftly explained the basis
> through scripture and interviews. His meticulous re-
> search should make even the staunchest critic apprecia-
> tive of his premise – especially the way he manages to
> weave the Holy Spirit, and thus the Trinity, into the inner
> workings of Judaism."
> —Dean Lee Coppola, Jandoli School of Journalism,
> St. Bonaventure University

Searching for Jesus in the Jewish Mind: The Unseen Hand of God

> "Anthony Cardinale is a gifted journalist and author who
> has immersed himself for over 30 years in a move of God
> that is for the most part unknown to most Christians.
> I'm referring to a promise God made throughout the
> Scriptures to restore the Jewish People to Himself at a set
> time in history (Jeremiah 31:33–34). Anthony is in the
> forefront of this revival."
> —Rabbi Jonathan Bernis, Jewish Voice Ministries,
> International

THE BEAUTIFUL LAND THAT EVERYBODY COVETS

Up the Mediterranean coast, from Tel Aviv to Netanya and on to Haifa and the Lebanese border, travelers see the terrain, soil and vegetation go through every conceivable variation in less than two hours. Dairy cattle graze on flatlands next to fields of roses. Around Hadera come lush fruit gardens. Abruptly, the Mediterranean comes into full view on the left, and desert dunes on the right. Then wide, flat farmlands under cultivation, with picturesque mountains in the background. The smell of fertilizer prickles the nostrils, and a creek runs across the landscape, followed by fields of palm trees.

Back in Jerusalem, an old Arab slowly leads his donkey laden with sacks of cement through Jaffa Gate into Old City. From the tower of the domed mosque near the Wailing Wall, the Muslim *muezzin* calls the hour of daily prayer in Arabic over a loudspeaker.

In the shops and outdoor bazaars, Arab dealers haggle with customers over the price of a wicker basket, or a brass candlestick, or a handful of dates. An Arab boy offers his services as a guide; he can adapt his spiel to the Christian looking for the Holy Sepulchre or the Jewish visitors looking for David's tomb.

A Jewish boy begs me for money for his sister's wedding, but I don't believe him and jump on a bus. He chases the bus on his bike, and when it stops at my hotel he begs again; I laugh and give him five dollars.

An Arab boy pesters tourists to buy wooden animals or reed flutes at the top of the Mount of Olives, where Jesus once stood and beheld the panorama of the palms and flowers and walls surrounding the Temple and wept over the city.

This is the beautiful land that the Palestinian Jews and the Palestinian Arabs have been struggling over. And in these skies are the stars that shone on crystal clear nights for the prophets of all three faiths . . . over the desert where the soul, stripped of all its baggage, whispers truth.

ix

Author's Preface

THE REVOLT OF THE *Palestinian Jews* defends the historic right that Israelis have to the Land of Israel, despite the world's embrace of Arabs as the only "Palestinians"—many of them from families that emigrated from Arab countries after Jewish immigrants "made the desert bloom."

How the Netanyahu Government Invited the October 7 Massacre is explored, starting with the polarization of Israeli society that was exploited and exacerbated by the most radical ultra-nationalist and ultra-religious coalition in the Jewish state's history.

The book explores the origins and shocking extent of the "Palestinian Jewish Revolt," as I call it, by the Benjamin Netanyahu government. In its attempt to reclaim western Palestine for the Palestinian Jews, it promulgated anti-Arab policies that seemed designed to provoke a Palestinian-Arab intifada that might provide an excuse to expel some or all Arabs from Gaza and the West Bank.

Only after the demise of this Netanyahu coalition could *the real Israel* stand again proudly before the world.

The purpose of this book is to clarify the underlying reality of Israel's Palestinian Jews, vis a vis the Palestinian Arabs, and then to trace the historic causes of this nativist, ultra-nationalist, ultra-religious movement . . . and lament where it might be going.

Drawing on seeds planted in 2012 in my first book, *The Red Heifer: A Jewish Cry for Messiah,* I now bring them to fruition as Israel takes this bold turn in the direction of a rabbinic theocracy

1

(Chapter 4, "Zionism Goes Ultra-Religious"). Next comes a chapter on the mentor of this Palestinian Jewish Revolt, Rabbi Meir Kahane, whom I interviewed several years before he was assassinated by an Arab. His anti-Arab legacy lives on in Israel.

A sympathetic chapter on how the Palestinian Arabs have "No Place to Call Their Own" is followed by a brief but shocking summary of the atrocities of October 7. . . and this observation:

Hamas seems pleased that tens of thousands of its civilians have been killed during the Israel Defense Forces' counter-offensive in Gaza—and that most of the infrastructure has been decimated by the bombing. After using them as human shields, it now is clear that Hamas is willing to sacrifice not only the lives of its own people (honoring them as heaven-bound "martyrs") but even the future livability of the Gaza Strip—because its eyes are on the real prize: "All of Palestine, from the river to the sea."

To that end, the sadistic barbarism inflicted on its victims were meant to strike terror into Israelis and encourage their exodus from the Holy Land.

A bright note comes in the next chapter, as I share a poignant experience I had in Bethlehem, where I witnessed the Jew and Arab working together as brothers in Christ. This is the only answer to the turmoil between Jews and Arabs in the resurrected State of Israel.

After tracing the rise of Christian Zionism since the 1967 Mideast War—when Israel recovered Jerusalem, the West Bank and Gaza—I conclude with a prediction about the final, divine polarization in human history as God sifts the tares from the wheat in the Holy Land. I pose a bold question: Is it possible that the dangerous agenda of Netanyahu's far-right coalition—exploiting this *ungodly* polarization—reflects the will of God—who has repeatedly asserted in Scripture his desire to separate the tares from the wheat and force everyone to openly stand for or against God? I call this the *godly* polarization for the final days.

Along the way are my frequent reminders of God's command to the Jews (36 times in the Pentateuch) to treat fairly the strangers living in their midst . . . particularly since recovering their ancient homeland in 1948 (and Jerusalem, Judea and Samaria in 1967).

Over the years, during my travels in Israel, I have noticed a heart-breaking change in Israeli society. Israelis once were super-patriotic, often spontaneously breaking out and singing "Ha Tikva" or "Jerusalem of Gold" on their plane as it was landing in Tel Aviv, or even on a bus during rush hour traffic. Since then, Israelis (like Americans) have become polarized over political and religious issues, to the point of demonizing one another in public.

Thus was born an ungodly polarization—as opposed to the divine polarization that I'll be discussing at the end of the book.

During one of my many stays in Jerusalem, I was granted a residency in 1998 at Mishkenot Sha'ananim, the city's guest house for visiting writers and artists, with its iconic windmill. There I researched my first book, *The Red Heifer: A Jewish Cry for Messiah*. In fact, the current search for a red heifer was an astonishing factor in Hamas's motives on October 7, 2023. The ashes of a female cow with rust-red but no white or black hairs are required (see Nu 19:5) for purification before the Temple can be rebuilt on the Temple Mount. That's where the Muslim golden Dome of the Rock now stands. . . not far from the massive Al-Aqsa mosque, which IDF police stormed during Ramadan on April 5, 2023, precipitating a riot.

Always protective of the Al-Aqsa mosque, Hamas feels threatened that Israelis are raising five Red Angus heifers imported from Texas, hoping one of them will retain its all-red coat to be slaughtered and burned on the Mount of Olives, its ashes of purification to be sprinkled over the priests and construction workers for the new Temple.

Those five heifers were the subject of a televised speech on January 14, 2024 by Abu Obeida, the military spokesman for the Hamas Al-Qassam Brigades. "We look back 100 days," he began—calling on Arabs to remember the Israeli raid on the Al-Aqsa mosque—and condemning certain Orthodox Jews for the "bringing of red cows as an application of a detestable religious myth designed for aggression against the feelings of an entire nation in the heart of its Arab identity, and the path of its prophet (the Night Journey) and Ascension to heaven."[1]

Those heifers, then, must be destroyed.

As a Christian Zionist who has interviewed Palestinian Arab refugees in Jordan as well as Israel over the years, I know that the hatred fomented by Arab leaders among their people has made it impossible for a peaceful solution to the Arab-Israeli conflict. But the Bible says that the God of Israel wants these Jewish and Arab cousins—descendants of Isaac and Ishmael—to embrace each other and live together in peace. It looks like this can only happen after the second coming of Messiah Yeshua.

—Anthony Cardinale

1. Obeida, "One Hundredth Day of War"

1

Did the Netanyahu Government Invite the October 7 Massacre?

They have said, "Come, and let us cut them off from being a nation, that the name of Israel may be remembered no more."

—Ps 83:4

THE BIBLE PREDICTS THAT in the final days the nations will attack Israel, bringing about Jacob's Trouble and the Great Tribulation. But it doesn't tell us why, after hating the Jews since time immemorial, the nations will suddenly find an excuse to attack and destroy the Jewish state.

That excuse may well be Israel's response to the latest and most serious attack on its people since the Holocaust, and the suspicion that Israel intends to drive all the Arabs out of Gaza.

The October 7 attack by Hamas was the most devastating confirmation possible of the warnings I was writing about in this book at the time—that the reckless anti-Arab policies of the Benjamin Netanyahu government would increase antisemitism and possibly provoke a regional war.

The *anti-Zionism* that had been steadily rising under Netanyahu during the first nine months of 2023 had now morphed into a worldwide outbreak of *antisemitism*, the likes of which this generation had never before seen.

To what extent was the savage genocidal butchery from Gaza provoked by the actions of the Benjamin Netanyahu government over the previous nine months?

No, this is not to blame Zionism or "the occupation" for what happened, as much of the world claims. It is to examine whether the actions of one Israeli career politician, who was on trial in three corruption cases—and who made himself hostage to a coalition of heartless right-wing politicians in hopes of decriminalizing the charges against him—contributed to Hamas's decision to attack Israel, slaughtering some 1,200 Israelis and taking more than 300 hostages. If this had happened in America, the proportional death toll would have been 36,000 lives.

The new government encouraged the attacks on Palestinian Arab communities in the West Bank by religious Israeli settlers—who, if they had been true to their faith, would have been reaching out to their Ishmaelite cousins in their midst in a sincere attempt to foster a peaceful coexistence. If the mistreatment of those Arab refugees were to reach a boiling point, Israel's nearly two million Arab citizens might well rise up and engulf the entire nation in a civil war.

Then came the horrendous death toll among Arab civilians living in Gaza as the IDF bombed thousands of targets in preparation for a ground invasion to rescue hostages and wipe out Hamas. The world will never forget those scenes of parents clinging to their dying or dead children amid the rubble that evinced an apocalyptic catastrophe. Nor will it ever forgive Israel for this supposed "genocide"—although I must add that Netanyahu's most rabid partners weren't bothered by the death toll in Gaza, hoping to evict its occupants and resettle it with Jews. Again, only after the departure of those partners in the government could the *real* Israel stand proudly again before the world.

Months after the Israel Defense Forces campaign began, terrorists in Gaza continued to bombard Israeli civilians with rockets daily—while Hezbollah in Lebanon bombarded northern Israel daily, indefinitely displacing 100,000 Israelis from their homes. And Hamas boasted of plans to repeat the October 7 atrocities again and again until they "cut them off from being a nation, that the name of Israel may be remembered no more."

But how quickly the world dismissed or forgot the scenes of Israeli civilians slaughtered by Hamas death squads (See chapter on "What Some Palestinian Arabs Did to Palestinian Jews"). On college campuses, decades of indoctrination by liberal professors bore bitter fruit as gullible students, who were never taught critical thinking in grammar and high school, demonstrated by the thousands not just for the Palestinian Arabs but for the terrorist organization Hamas. The Marxist teaching that divides humans between the oppressor and the oppressed has denied Jews their history of being the oppressed, recasting them as part of the white oppressors against Arabs and other people of color.

As for being guilty of "colonialism" in Palestine, the Jews fleeing the Holocaust were not coming to Palestine as settlers to create a colony on behalf of a home country back in Europe. They had no home country (except the Holy Land). It would be just as absurd to accuse Arabs of colonialism for emigrating to western Palestine in order to share the economic benefits that Jews were bringing to the land in the years leading up to 1948.

As the months went by, anti-Jewish student protests swelled into the hundreds of thousands, as students formed encampments at scores of university campuses across the land, shutting down classes and terrorizing Jewish students physically, many chanting, "Death to the Jews!" Many faculty members joined in, some offering their students extra credit for participating. To them, colleges are here to *radicalize students as leftist political activists*, not *teach students* and prepare them to make their own political decisions about the left versus the right.

Americans were never reminded by the media that the protesters amounted to less than 1 percent of each college's students.

I'd like to ask each pro-Hamas student if he or she is a Christian. Then I would point out that Jesus was a Jew and will continue to practice his Jewish faith, such as observing the Passover, when he returns. At the Last Supper he told his disciples:

> "I have eagerly desired to eat this Passover with you before I suffer, for I tell you, I shall not eat it [again] until there is fulfillment in the kingdom of God."
> —Luke 22:1516 (NAB)

The thousands of civilian deaths and injuries in Gaza would certainly justify mass protests demanding a cease-fire, and I might have actually joined in. And I have to admire students who—no longer apathetic about world affairs—were willing to risk their college careers and be permanently suspended for the cause of the Gazans. But why couldn't they have limited their ire to Netanyahu and his corrupt government in Israel? Why did they have to target all Jews, most of whom have never even been to Israel, and many of them on the Palestinian Arabs' side, even joining the demonstrations as Jews?

In loudly supporting Hamas, these students ignored the fact that those terrorists had deliberately targeted civilians—while every civilian death in Gaza was collateral and unintended by the Israel Defense Forces. Nor were they troubled that Hamas terrorists rejected negotiations to release civilian hostages . . . threatening to carry out genocidal massacres in Israel again and again . . . and hijacking truckloads of humanitarian food and fuel, squirreling it underground for themselves, the better to perpetuate indefinitely the suffering of their people, suffering that they themselves had caused in the past.

Sensing this, right-wing settlers in the West Bank blocked an aid convey heading to Gaza on May 13, 2024, spilled the trucks' cargo onto the road, and set two trucks on fire. Four of them were arrested.

Many outside agitators with no connection to the colleges infiltrated the encampments, whose tents were paid for by left-wing organizations, such as billionaire George Soros' Open Society Foundation.

And the protesters' silence about the suffering and fate of the hostages in Gaza was deafening. In fact, many students were spitefully tearing down photos of the Israeli hostages!

Meanwhile, rockets continued to be fired from Gaza (as well as Lebanon) months after the IDF began its assault.

October 7 and its aftermath will go down as an awesome turning point in human history, accelerating the international conditions necessary for the final days. Many Christians believe that this perhaps *final* wave of global antisemitism is a desperate demonic sign of the final days, with Israel's unpopular war against Hamas foreshadowing the coming Battle of Armageddon (Rev 16:16). The Bible predicts that multiple nations will attack Israel, but it is unclear what crime they will accuse the hated Jewish state of having committed.

Benjamin Netanyahu & Co. have given the world a possible excuse. He returned to office as prime minister in late 2022 by assembling the most radical coalition of right-wing parties in the nation's history. There followed a continuous flow of actions that seemed designed to provoke Arabs living in the "West Bank" (Samaria and Judea)—heedless of the danger of arousing Israel's nearly two million Arab citizens to attack their Jewish neighbors as they had in May of 2021.

Such an uprising could explode into a third war front, in addition to Hamas in Gaza to the southwest and Hezbollah in Lebanon to the north.

True, many factors contributed to Hamas's decision to mount such a bold, unprecedented attack on Israel, sparking its fifth war with Israel over the past 15 years. Hamas was alarmed when the cause of the Palestinian Arabs had been ignored as several Arab countries created ties with Israel under the Abraham Accords—and Saudi Arabia was about to do likewise. But if the policies of the Netanyahu government had even a minor role in provoking the attack, they might have brought it all to the tipping point.

They were an open invitation to attack a historically divided people.

The bloody invasion by some 3,000 terrorists from Gaza was covertly planned for many months, during the rising tide of anti-Arab provocations by the more racist members of Bibi's coalition. Even if the original idea for some sort of sneak attack was seeded earlier in the minds of Israel's enemies, they were emboldened by what Netanyahu & Co. were doing throughout 2023. To Hamas, Israel was permanently altering the status quo, leaving the terrorist organization no choice but to fight back in a brutally dramatic way that might draw the Arab world into a war with Israel.

Hamas seems pleased that tens of thousands of its civilians have been killed during the Israel Defense Forces' counter-offensive in Gaza—and that most of the infrastructure has been decimated by the bombing. After using them as human shields, it now is clear that Hamas is willing to sacrifice not only the lives of its own people (honoring them as heaven-bound "martyrs") but even the future livability of the Gaza Strip—because its eyes are on the real prize: "All of Palestine, from the river to the sea."

The world somehow expects Israel to care more about the Arabs in Gaza than Hamas does.

The terrorist death squads slaughtered entire families in their beds, cribs and wheelchairs; raped mothers while burning their children in ovens; beheaded babies in front of their parents; raped and beheaded young girls, and threw grenades into bomb shelters packed with terrified civilians.

This genocidal attack came at a time of ungodly polarization in Israeli society. As syndicated columnist David Ignatius of the Washington Post Writers Group wrote four days later:

"Israel seemed to be coming apart in the months before Hamas fighters broke through the Gaza cage. Thousands of Israelis were marching in the streets of Tel Aviv to protest Netanyahu's attempt to alter what they saw as the fundamental character of the state. Did that political chaos contribute to the Gaza attacks? I don't know. But, surely, the domestic feuds of the past few months might have led Hamas and its backers in Tehran to believe that Israel was internally weak and, perhaps, vulnerable." [1]

1. Ignatius, "As Gaza War Enters"

A member of Netanyahu's government resigned in protest shortly after October 7. Public Diplomacy Minister Galit Distel Atbaryan finally made a public statement on November 16, saying: "The bottom line is, we were at the helm and the country is in a terrible state. We certainly bear responsibility—that's why I resigned right after the heavy shake-up of that black Saturday. . . The days of this government are numbered, that's obvious. I hope that out of the destruction something newer and healthy will be established, otherwise we are done for."[2]

David Halperin, CEO of the Israel Policy Forum, wrote: "For nearly a year, my colleagues and I at the Israel Policy Forum have joined with others in expressing concern about the nature of Israel's far-right government. . . Our hope, alongside so many others, was that a government influenced by inexperienced, far-right leaders would not be tasked with managing a security crisis, let alone one of this magnitude."[3]

The October 7 butchery was bad enough. But no one could have predicted how it would energize those who hate Zionism, and how Israel's retaliation would be met with worldwide protests supporting not only the Arabs in Gaza, but Hamas itself. No longer could anyone say that anti-Zionism was not antisemitism. It was as if millions of latent Jew haters had been waiting years for such an opportunity as this to crawl out of the woodwork and demand death to all Jews.

And it began immediately on October 7, *before* the world would see pictures of Arabs dying during the IDF's entry into Gaza.

Particularly on college campuses, students who had never been taught critical thinking had been indoctrinated with the Marxist principle that capitalist society is divided between the oppressors and their oppressed victims. Idealistic young people also are prone to root for the perceived underdog. They ignored the gory details of the demonic slaughter carried out by 3,000 terrorists, many of them cowards hyped up on drugs. These gullible students immediately cried out that the Israelis had brought this on

2. Atbaryan, "Former Minister"
3. Halperin, Israel Policy Forum

themselves by their treatment of "the Palestinians" (meaning the Palestinian Arabs, as opposed to the Palestinian Jews; see Chapter 3, "What About the Palestinian Jews?").

How bad must an atrocity be for such students to put aside their political views for a moment and speak out against the reprehensible excesses of their political heroes? Idealistic young people who are incapable of critical thinking are not yet college material. They should stay away from the toxic college classroom for their own good.

As for the people of Gaza, one might ask how much they must suffer the consequences of their leaders' hatred of Israel and Jews before rising up against Hamas.

During the years when so many Palestinian Arabs blew themselves up in order to murder Israeli civilians, none apparently were willing to go on a suicide mission to rid themselves of a top Hamas leader. Nor had they become disenchanted after being used as human shields by cowardly Hamas leaders, who even dug elaborate command control centers under Gaza hospitals, one of them for children.

Yet Hamas terrorists had plenty of time on their hands—not to work for a living and support their families but to dig miles of tunnels over the course of several years.

"The tunnels in Gaza were built to protect Hamas fighters, not civilians," a Hamas officer, Mousa Abu Marzouk, said during an interview on Arabic TV on November 1, 2023. "Protecting Gaza civilians is the responsibility of the UN and Israel."[4]

Ironically, the United Nations Relief and Work Agency for Palestine Refugees in the Near East (UNRWA) headquarters in Gaza was harboring an underground tunnel used by Hamas as an intelligence hub, *run by electricity from the agency.* And a dozen UNRWA employees had actually taken part in the October 7 violence in Israel. Several of the Israeli hostages were held by UNRWA employees in their homes in Gaza.

The European Parliament has condemned the Palestinian Authority and its longtime enabler, UNRWA, for the hate-filled

4. Marzouk, Arabic TV

school books and learning materials that contributed to the October 7 massacre and the war in Gaza. It called for the EU to freeze its educational funding until school books are free of antisemitism and incitement to violence. One reason Arab countries won't accept Palestinian Arab refugees is because they have been so indoctrinated since childhood in UNRWA schools.

"Several generations of Gazans have been born and raised in the territory since the War of Independence in 1948, yet they still have refugee status," writes Alex Winston of the *International Jerusalem Post.* "Millions of Palestinians have been granted Jordanian and Lebanese citizenship over the years, yet they are still considered refugees by the international community."[5]

While the world was crying "collective punishment!" about the multitudes of civilian casualties in Gaza, claiming that they were helpless wards of Hamas, a sobering reminder was published by David M. Weinberg in the *International Jerusalem Post.* "Broadly speaking, Hamas does faithfully reflect the desires and goals of most Palestinians in Gaza," he wrote, "otherwise, it would not have been elected [by them] and been able to draft tens of thousands of jihadists into its military.

"Thousands of ordinary Palestinians," Weinberg continued, "carried out the worst atrocities of the Simchat Torah (October 7) massacre. Tens of thousands have participated in riots on border fences going back years (which apparently served as cover for assault planning). The 'uninvolved' danced like dervishes around the trucks that hauled away the abducted men, women and children of Kibbutz Be'eri, crying, 'Death to the Jews' while helping Hamas hide them. 'Uninvolved' mothers proclaim they are proud to send their children into battle to turn them into *shahids* (martyrs). And 'uninvolved' teachers teach the children of Gaza that it's a religious obligation and heroic task to kill Jews. The 'uninvolved' have helped Hamas hide its rocket launchers and other weapons, too."[6]

(Weinberg is founding senior fellow at the Misgav Institute for National Security and Zionist Strategies, an Israeli think tank

5. Winston, "A Man on a Mission," 18
6. Weinberg, "Enough Truce," 20

with ties to Israeli Prime Minister Benjamin Netanyahu. It issued a report on October 17 promoting the "unique and rare opportunity" for the "relocation and final settlement of the entire Gaza population.")

Despite their failure to rise up against Hamas, the heartbreaking suffering of Gazans during the Israeli assault must have given many Palestinian Arabs a sense of deja vu and disillusionment over the consequences of supporting the Hamas leadership for so many years. British Palestinian writer John Aziz wrote an article in the *Atlantic* about how "violence fail[ed] the Palestinian cause," under the headline: "All My Life, I've Watched Violence Fail the Palestinian Cause."[7]

Weeks before October 7, a public-opinion poll conducted by Arab Barometer found that a majority of Gazans did not support Hamas but favored a peaceful settlement with Israel. However, a poll conducted in late November by Palestinian-Arab scholar and analyst Khalil Shikaki found that support had kicked up since October 7.[8]

But some short clips published in February 2024 on "Gaza's Liberators," an anti-Hamas Telegram channel, showed people chanting slogans against Hamas leaders and shouting, "Bring down Hamas!" in Rafah, the southern town where a million displaced Gazans were sheltering. Clips filmed in Jabaliya, in the north, showed Hamas opening fire on demonstrators, killing one and seriously wounding three.[9]

Rafah—where thousands of remaining terrorists were holed up with their leaders—would soon draw world condemnation as Israel prepared a ground assault in the midst of more than a million Gazan refugees sheltering there in tents with nowhere to flee for safety or to get food. In Rafah, Hamas was again using its own people as human shields. The United Nations warned of an impending catastrophe, while Arab nations charged Israel with "starvation

7. Aziz, "All My Life"

8. Jamal, and Robbins, "What Palestinians Really Think of Hamas"

9. "Ahrar Gaza on Telegram"

warfare." By mid-May, about 800,000 of them had somehow made their way out of Rafah, stumbling to the decimated north.

But did Hamas really want a cease-fire?

"Precipitating a massive Israeli operation in Rafah would be worth the cost, because it would isolate Israel globally and deepen the U.S.-Israeli divide," suggested Jon B. Alterman, director of the Middle East program at the Center for Strategic and International Studies in Washington.

Did Bibi really want such a cease-fire?

"Netanyahu needs the Rafah operation to remain in power and to appease the fanatics in his coalition. Bottom line, Netanyahu has little to gain from a cease-fire deal and a lot to lose," said Khaled Elgindy, a senior fellow at the Middle East Institute and former advisor to Arab peace negotiators.[10]

In May 2024 Bibi became the first prime minister of Israel to stubbornly provoke her American ally to suspend shipments of bombs. President Joseph Biden said he didn't want 2,000-pound American-made bombs to be used to kill civilians in Rafah. Bibi ignored the warning. (Back in 1982, President Ronald Reagan had threatened to withhold cluster bombs, but Prime Minister Menachem Begin immediately halted use of them in the war in Lebanon.)

From the very beginning, Netanyahu & Co. were guilty of setting the stage for the devastating security failure on October 7. Yet the writing was clearly on the wall. A week before the attack, Seth J. Frantzman wrote in the *International Jerusalem Post* : "Over the last week, the IDF noted increased incidents along the Gaza border" and speculating that "Rioting along the Gaza border fence . . . could indicate its intentions there."[11]

In fact, three months before the invasion, IDF surveillance soldiers observed unusual Hamas training exercises. Some time later, senior officers in the IDF dismissed as "fantasies" the warnings they received from two lower-level officers in the elite intelligence unit about Hamas' preparations for a mass invasion of Israel.

10. Baker, "Scramble to Broker a Gaza Deal," A-7

11. Frantzman, "Hamas Is Fueling," 5

One of the junior officers reported that the Hamas drill included the use of vehicles to carry out an attack and practiced taking over Israeli towns—adding that the attack was on such a large scale that it could spark an all-out war. After being briefed, a senior officer agreed that the information was substantial but that Hamas wasn't capable of carrying such a large-scale attack.[12]

Then, on December 10 came Bradley Burston's new book, *The End of Israel: Dispatches from a Path to Catastrophe,* cinching the case that Netanyahu knew long before October 7 that something dangerous was taking place in Gaza.

"He was specifically warned, and the warnings got worse as the year went on," he wrote. "There were public statements made throughout the year, some by recently retired generals warning of that perfect storm brewing." [13]

If a politically moderate government had emerged from the elections in late 2022, a prime minister with integrity could have reined in the settlers who were murdering Arabs in the West Bank and burning their crops and homes in attempts to drive them from the Holy Land. Such a government would have also been more cautious in dealing with Hamas's infiltration of the West Bank. Instead, the government exhibited a reckless disregard for the possibility of provoking a third front in the West Bank, in addition to a two-front war against Hamas in the southwest and Hezbollah in the north.

"Military analysts said the Israeli army had enough troops to wage the ground offensive [in Gaza] while carrying out regular operations in the West Bank," Mark Landler and Ronen Bergman of the *New York Times* reported. "But it would be outstretched if it were to carry out a parallel offensive in the West Bank, according to Yagil Levy, an expert on the Israeli military at the Open University of Israel." The article continued:

"'The army should have calmed down the West Bank,' Levy said. "'But they've lost much of their control there.' Since Oct. 7, violence by settlers in the West Bank has displaced more than 800

12. "IDF Elite Intel Officer"
13. Burston, *End of Israel*

Palestinians." The West Bank—the so-called "occupied Palestinian territory"—is the home of about 500,000 Jewish settlers and 2.7 million Arabs, most of them refugees from the 1948 and 1967 wars. It was not a "Palestinian territory" before the twentieth century, but it had been the heart of Israel 2,000 years ago.[14]

A more worthy prime minister also would have rejected Benjamin Netanyahu's longtime strategy of exploiting the divisions in Israeli society for personal political gain. Netanyahu had never favored a two-state solution (nor do I), despite his public lip service. And now his dream coalition had mounted what I would call a "Palestinian Jewish Revolt" against Palestinian Arabs, having grown tired of sharing the Jewish homeland with them.

Netanyahu's culpability for the Gaza massacre may even extend back to 2010, when he succeeded Ehud Olmert as prime minister. Olmert had attempted to work out a peace deal with the Palestinian Authority that included Gaza, where Hamas had violently ejected the Palestinian Authority in 2007, throwing PA officials off rooftops.

"Netanyahu, a reckless and cynical leader, sought to strengthen Hamas's position in Gaza," according to an article in *Foreign Affairs* three weeks after the Hamas attack. "He espoused the ill-fated notion that Hamas's rule in Gaza was fundamentally good for Israel: Israeli interests were better served by Palestinian disunity—with Gaza split from the West Bank, where the moderate PA holds sway—than by political unity among Palestinians." [15]

Christians and religious Jews have asked why God allowed this barbaric genocidal attack on October 7 to happen. Was it to awaken nonreligious Israeli Jews from their apostasy against traditional family structure and against the unborn?

> "Oh, that My people would listen to Me,
> that Israel would walk in My ways!
> I would soon subdue their enemies. . ."
> —Ps 81:13–14

14. Landler and Bergman, "As Gaza War Enters"

15. Aylan, Sher and Petruschka, "Why Netanyahu Must Go"

Nearly 400 young Israelis were butchered at the Nova Music Festival, a night of music and dancing in the desert in southern Israel. "The party-goers had erected a giant statue of Buddha in the central pavilion around which they dance all night," wrote Gil Afriat, a Messianic Jew with Tiferet Yeshiva Congregation in Tel Aviv. "Many in Israel who saw that blatant display of idolatry did the quick arithmetic of: *'God is judging the hedonistic, secular Israelis for the sin of idolatry.'* Many believers here in the Land viewed October 7 as God's judgment of the sins of secular Israel, such as abortion, immorality, and materialism."[16]

Or could it have been God's way of bringing back together Israel's polarized society by uniting Israelis against a common enemy? The Talmud says God allowed the destruction of the Temple and eviction of the Jews from Palestine because of their words and actions of hatred toward each other. So, ungodly polarization among Jews goes back more than two millennia.

The atrocities during the October 7 massacre certainly brought Israelis—both religious and secular—back together to face this existential threat to the Jewish state. Time would tell how long it would last.

16. Afriat, "October 7 and John 7," 7

2

An Ungodly Polarization

WEARY OF HEARING PALESTINIAN Arabs universally referred to as "the Palestinians," I undertook an exploration of how many of their families had actually emigrated to Palestine from other Middle East countries—and how Israeli Jews have a much more authentic claim to the Holy Land and should be recognized as "Palestinian Jews."

Then, after the November 2022 elections in Israel, I coined the term "Palestinian Jewish Revolt" to describe the nativist, ultra-religious coalition of Benjamin Netanyahu. Many of his partners seemed intent on claiming Israeli Jews' full inheritance of the land by openly provoking Palestinian Arabs, even at the risk of sparking a third intifada, or worse—the October 7, 2023 attack from Gaza that slaughtered hundreds of Israelis and created an existential threat to the future of the Jewish state.

Prime Minister Netanyahu's latest government was able to attract only radical religious parties to his coalition because his previous partners refused to work with a prime minister on trial on several serious charges of political corruption. After he took office and initiated a "judicial reform"—at first proposing that the Knesset could overturn the Supreme Court's rulings by a simple majority vote—hundreds of thousands of Israelis demonstrated for several weeks. Many of them accused him of plotting to have the Knesset decriminalize the offenses for which he was standing trial.

"Bibi," as he is affectionately (or ruefully) called, "in an apparent effort to avoid conviction in his ongoing corruption trials, is trying to destroy the independence of the Israeli courts, and pandering to ultra-radical cabinet ministers who guarantee him the votes to do so," columnist Trudy Rubin of the *Philadelphia Inquirer* wrote seven months before the massacre. "Bibi's attention appears focused mainly on saving his own skin."[1]

In fact, the Knesset soon passed a law blocking the Supreme Court from ordering the prime minister to recuse himself from office due to a conflict of interest. In January 2024, the High Court determined that it had been passed to personally benefit the premier. The court postponed its implementation until after the next election when a new prime minister, not necessarily Bibi, would enjoy its protection.

Thousands of Netanyahu's supporters took to the streets, clashing with the demonstrators, prompting President Isaac Herzog to express fears of a civil war. The last civil war among the Jews ended with their expulsion by the Romans in 70 AD.

This ungodly polarization not only endangered democracy in Israel, but it also made the Jewish state vulnerable in the eyes of her enemy—who struck ten months later on October 7. (Yet the day will come when God allows a divine polarization—between faithful and unfaithful Jews—to separate the tares from the wheat in the last days; see final chapter, "God's Plan to Sift the Tares from the Wheat.")

The radicals sought to neuter the Supreme Court by "judiciary reform," based on claims that unelected judges had ruled too often in discrimination suits for Arab citizens as well as Arabs living in the contested West Bank. The reform's most ardent supporters are Orthodox Jews who fear the Court might strip them of their favors under Netanyahu's past governments, including immunity from military duty and continuation of family welfare support while the men spend their days studying the Talmud.

1. Rubin, "Netanyahu's Attack on Israel's Judiciary"

In addition, the courts until now had frequently irked the religious leaders by granting Messianic Jews certain equal rights, such as freedom of expression and religious assembly, in the face of sometimes violent attacks by the Orthodox.

No matter what the future would hold for Netanyahu's coalition, or its reckless brinkmanship, nothing could undo the damage to democracy in Israel. The coalition leaders poisoned the people with distrust of their institutions by making the government hostage to religious radicals who would resort to violent disruption for the sake of flexing their newfound muscles. If Netanyahu were to allow this fervor to infect Israel's foreign policy, many said, we might see a regional war break out.

As it is, the October 7 invasion of Israel from Gaza was intended by Hamas to draw Arab nations and Hezbollah in Lebanon into a regional war of annihilation of the Jewish state. In fact, before the October 7 attack, Yahya Sinwar, the Hamas leader in Gaza, had obtained a commitment from Hezbollah to launch a joint attack on Israel. But even after the IDF had committed between 30,000 and 40,000 of its troops to Gaza, Hezbollah fired rockets daily into Israel but delayed an all-out assault indefinitely.

Hamas's hope for a regional war against Israel seemed about to be realized, when the Houthis in Yemen began launching drones against the Jewish state—and when Iran fired 350 drones and ballistic and cruise missiles into Israel on April 13, 2024, in retaliation for the bombing of Iran's embassy in Damascus, Syria, killing seven top leaders. The bombardment on April 13 was an embarrassing failure for Iran, as half of the ballistic missiles fell short of Israeli territory and nearly every projectile that actually made it to Israel was shot down by Israel and the U.S. Navy ships in the eastern Mediterranean, with aid of the British and Jordanians.

Most importantly, no lives were lost.

Remarkably, neighboring Sunni Arab countries gave strategic assistance that day to Israel against the Shi'ite regime of Iran, which they fear and despise.

In retaliation, Israel at first considered a wide counter-strike on military targets but instead fired a single missile at the radar system protecting the Natanz nuclear facilities—sending a message that Israel could reach out and touch Iran—and avoiding an escalation of hostilities.

Now, the mentor of the radicals in Netanyahu's government was the late Rabbi Meir Kahane, who wanted to blow up the Dome of the Rock and rebuild the Temple there. During a private interview with Kahane during his heyday, I asked him if he feared sparking World War III. "It would bring the Messiah," he replied. I was shocked by his seriousness.

The coalition's most radical extremists were most intent on preventing the establishment of a Palestinian state in the Holy Land. No doubt they also harbored visions of someday expelling all Arabs from the West Bank (and eventually Gaza). If that was the case, then the October 7 attack gave them a perfect excuse not only to destroy Hamas, but to drive every Arab out of Gaza by leveling the land for the ground invasion.

But what about the nearly two million Arab citizens of Israel whose families never fled in 1948 or 1967? Many of them still refuse to vote in national elections, lest they appear to accept the status quo and Israeli rule. But they enjoy the protection of the courts and, according to polls, would rather live under Israeli rule than under an Islamist regime. Arab citizens are in the Knesset, on the Supreme Court, many of them doctors, lawyers and other professionals, even police officers.

Extremists in the coalition seemed to have forgotten how Arab citizens of Israel had risen up against their Jewish neighbors in defense of their brothers and sisters in the "occupied" West Bank in May 2021. Riots, set off by provocative police interventions at the Al-Aqsa mosque, exposed seething resentments between Israel's Jewish and Arab citizens. *The New York Times* reported: "Across almost all of Israel's seven officially 'mixed' Arab-Jewish towns, gunfire, arson, stone-throwing and lynching left a trail of destruction. Arab mobs burned Jewish stores to the ground. Rightist Jewish vigilantes chanted 'Death to Arabs.'"[2]

2. "Israeli-Palestinian Hostilities"

Russell A. Shalev, a lawyer and researcher in the Legal Department of the Kohelet Policy Forum, wrote in *Fathom* journal in March 2022: "In little more than a week in May 2021, Arab rioters [who were Israeli citizens] set ablaze 10 synagogues and 112 Jewish residences, looted 386 Jewish homes and damaged another 673, and set 849 Jewish cars on fire. There were also 5,018 recorded instances of Jews being stoned. Three Jews were murdered and more than 600 were hurt. Over 300 police officers were injured in disturbances in over 90 locations across the country."[3]

Thus, Israel's nearly two million Arab citizens have the potential of sparking a nationwide civil war throughout Israel if they are sufficiently provoked by the government's incursions on the rights of Arab refugees in Gaza and the West Bank.

Nevertheless, after reviewing all that has happened under the new regime, I have dared to raise this question: Is any of this a reflection of the will of God? Is it possible that something positive, no matter how painful, might come out of it? Yes, it sounds unthinkable. But in my final chapter I propose that a spiritual sifting is going on in Israel today, as the God of Israel prepares the Chosen People for Messiah's coming. God is pressuring Israeli Jews to take a stand on the Torah, in order to separate those who truly love God from those who persist in their secular delusions.

The rabbis say that Messiah will come when the world is either entirely righteous or entirely wicked. If all are wicked, there will no longer be any reason for Messiah to delay coming and judging the world. If all are righteous, Messiah must immediately come and rule during a millennium of world peace.

I have asked several Orthodox rabbis whether there might be a third possibility in this "zero sum" game: What if the world were polarized between those fully religious and those stubbornly pagan who openly hate God, with nobody left sitting on the fence? Yes, the rabbis replied—this would bring Messiah.

And so, I have dared to ask whether the provocative actions of this Israeli government—or a future one—might also someday generate the conditions that will hasten the time of Jacob's Trouble

3. Shalev, "Israel Needs to Talk"

and the Great Tribulation. See Jeremiah 30:7—"Alas, what a terrible time of trouble it is! There has never been any like it. It is a time of trouble for the descendants of Jacob, but some of them will be rescued out of it." (NET)

Jesus spoke of this day as "a great tribulation, such as has not occurred since the beginning of the world until now, nor ever shall." (Matt 24:21, NKJ) In the final days, the nations will attack Israel. But why? What might the Jews of Israel do to provoke them? Perhaps by becoming a truly apartheid state and claiming the Holy Land as their own and expelling their Arab cousins, based on how God once drove the Canaanite pagans out of the land.

Only time will tell. . . .

3

What About the Palestinian Jews?

WHEN PEOPLE REFER TO "the Palestinians," they are specifying only Palestinian Arabs. But what about the other people living in the region called Palestine?

Would Norwegians dare to call themselves "*the* Scandinavians," ignoring the Swedes and the Danes who share that region?

There was never a country called Palestine, but for a thousand years there was a Jewish nation called Judea. Since the Roman expulsion of the Jews in 70 AD, the region has been known as Palestine.

Unlike the region called Scandinavia, which contains three nations, Palestine was an outlying, neglected region of the Turkish Ottoman Empire without any nations. That changed in the 1940s, with the rebirth of Israel (and the birth of Jordan). Those who insist on calling it only by the regional name of Palestine are denying the existence of the nation of Israel. . . and fabricating the existence "since time immemorial" of a people and a nation called Palestine.

In recent decades the word Palestinian was an adjective, not a noun—Palestinian Arab, Palestinian Christian, Palestinian Jew (Palestinian Talmud!). That changed in 1964, when the Palestine Liberation Organization was born, introducing to the world a new nationality called Palestinians. This was done simply by referring to Palestinian Arabs as "the Palestinians." These were Arabs who had become refugees in 1948 or 1967 after living *for various lengths of time* in Palestine.

But what about Palestinian Jews? The term sounds jarring. But the PLO itself has recognized such a people.

In July 1968, a year after Israel recovered the West Bank (ancient Samaria and Judea) and Gaza in the Six Day War, the PLO redrafted its Palestine National Covenant. Now it was rejecting any partition of Palestine between Arabs and Jews and calling for a single Arab state. The document recognized Palestinian Jews who "had normally resided in Palestine until the beginning of the Zionist invasion." Those pre-Zionist Jews would be allowed to continue to live as a minority in a future Palestinian state.

Would their children and grandchildren also qualify? After all, the children and grandchildren of Palestinian Arabs displaced in 1948 are also counted as refugees by the United Nations.

Many of the Arabs living as Israeli citizens—or living as refugees in the West Bank—are from families that were not natives of Palestine. We can also point to some 700,000 Jews who were forced to flee from Arab countries after Israel was reborn in 1948. They too were not natives of Palestine. But if those non-native Arabs can be called Palestinians, so can those non-native Jews, and their descendants.

If Sephardic Jews lived for a millennium as minorities in 22 Arab Muslim countries, why can't Palestinian Arabs live as minorities in the world's only Jewish state—a democratic state at that?

Since 700,000 is the estimated number of Arab departures as as well as Jewish arrivals, it can be viewed as "an exchange of refugees," Daniel Hannan writes in the *Washington Examiner*. He adds: "But whereas the displaced Jews became engaged Israeli citizens, the displaced Arabs have, tragically, become fourth-generation refugees."

Hannan also offers this breakdown of native Gazans versus refugees in Gaza: "Around 30% of Gazans, whose families were in the territory before the 1948 war, are considered native and are the responsibility of the local government—currently Hamas. The other 70% are treated as refugees, though few of them have seen the pre-1948 homes to which they lay claim. These are admin-istered by a special a special body," UNRWA. "Which brings us to the root of the problem. UNRWA's premise is that it is dealing with refugees, which implies that they will one day move to Israel. But that is not going to happen. Whatever land swaps accompany the establishment of an eventual Palestinian state, there will be no general right of return." [1]

∿

Following are my thoughts as a veteran journalist, after studying and visiting the Middle East for the past four decades. This book builds upon the themes I explored in my first book, *The Red Heifer: A Jewish Cry for Messiah*, and brings them up to date, with the benefit of a decade's hindsight.

During the British mandate over Palestine after the First World War, while Jewish immigrants from Europe were "illegally" entering the land formerly ruled by the Turkish Ottoman Empire, so were Arab immigrants doing so from Arab countries. These Arabs wished to take advantage of how the Jews were beginning to make the desert bloom.

Even after moving to Palestine, thousands of Arabs then moved from Arab settlements to Jewish settlements where the grass was greener.

Philip Hauser, director of the Population Research Center at the University of Chicago, described a study of census reports from the Turkish authorities, and later from the British authori-ties over Palestine. Between 1893 and 1947, an estimated 168,000 Arabs moved from Arab settlements to predominantly Jewish settlements within western Palestine. All of this is rather startling, in light of the repeated Arab claim that Jews arriving from Europe before, during and after the Holocaust had pushed Arabs out of their native soil.[2]

---

1. Hannan, "The Only Route to Peace in Gaza," 61
2. Peters, *Since Time Immemorial*, 428

Then, during the Second World War, thousands of laborers from Syria, Lebanon and Egypt were illegally brought into Palestine by "trucks" and by "train" to fill the "demand for labor exceeding the local supply," according to the Anglo-American Committee's 1945–46 *Survey of Palestine*. They were believed to have "remained in Palestine illegally." Other illegal immigrants came from Jordan, Persia, India, Somaliland, Abyssinia, and northwest Saudi Arabia.[3]

"The major increase in the population of the Arab villages in the coastal plain, during the British period, had come largely from immigrants from neighboring countries," according to Prof. Moshe Braver of Tel Aviv University, in his 1975 study titled, "Immigration as a Factor in the Growth of the Arab Village in Eretz-Israel." In one village, he found that "the great majority . . . had been born in Egypt."[4]

Even PLO leader Yasser Arafat was born in Egypt, yet he got away with calling himself a Palestinian.

In her classic, *From Time Immemorial*, Joan Peters describes a "carefully disguised Arab population increase by in-migration and illegal immigration." She revealed that in 1926 the British Controller of Permits for Jerusalem wrote: "It is agreed that refugees who would appear to be Syrian, Lebanese or Palestinian by nationality may be admitted into Palestine without passport or visa." In other words: *Come to Palestine and become a Palestinian.*

Peters added that British Colonial Secretary Malcolm McDonald once remarked: "If the Jews had not come to Palestine, the Arab population of Palestine would undoubtedly have remained fixed . . . where it had been for ages before."[5]

"Rather than a situation in which a teeming Arab people—present 'from time immemorial'—was forced off or excluded from its land, the situation is almost the exact opposite," Peters writes. "The Jews' land, earmarked as their Home [by Britain's Balfour

3. Peters, *From Time Immemorial.* 377–378

4. Braver, "Immigration as a Factor," 20

5. Peters, *Since Time Immemorial,* 339

Declaration], was usurped by the arrival of these Arab in-migrants from outside Jewish-settled areas" of Palestine.[6]

Peters also discovered that the United Nations had two definitions of "refugee" from 1948 on. "The more or less universally used description of eligibility included those people who were forced to leave 'permanent' or 'habitual' homes. In the case of the Arab refugees, however, the definition had been broadened to include as 'refugees' any persons who had been in 'Palestine' for only *two years* before Israel's statehood in 1948."[7]

After unearthing and studying population figures from when Palestine was a neglected outpost of the Ottoman Turkish Empire, Peters drew this interesting conclusion:

> We have seen strong evidence that the Holy Land was inhabited only sparsely in the nineteenth century. For centuries the non-Jewish, particularly the Muslim, peoples who did inhabit the land had been largely composed of a revolving immigrant population of diverse ethnic origins who could not possibly have constituted a substantial indigenous 'Palestinian' population, much less a nation of inhabitants for 'a thousand' or 'two thousand years.' Rather, the majority of those inhabitants were migrants and peasants originating from other lands.[8]

Meanwhile, the Jewish population was growing, and by 1850 Jews were the majority in Tiberias and Safed, and by the late 1850s they comprised at least half the population of Jerusalem. British Consul James Finn wrote in January 1856 that these mostly Sephardic Jews "greatly exceeded the Moslems in number."[9]

During the first half of the twentieth century, as Jews and Arabs continued to arrive, a demographic race was going on for the future control of the western Palestine (eastern Palestine is present-day Jordan, 70 percent of whose citizens are Palestinian Arabs).

6. Peters, *From Time Immemorial,* 249

7. Peters, *From Time Immemorial,* 4

8. Peters, *From Time Immemorial,* 196

9. Peters, *From Time Immemorial,* 199

However, not all Arab newcomers were unfriendly to the Palestinian Jews who had preceded them. In his book, *Army of Shadows: Palestinian Collaboration with Zionism, 1917–1948*, Hillel Cohen reveals the cooperation that early Zionists enjoyed with thousands of Arabs who had flocked to Palestine in the decades before 1948, eager to prosper in the shadow of the Jews who were establishing a thriving economy.[10]

"Hillel Cohen shows the crucial importance of Palestinian help to the Yishuv [the pre-state Jewish community]," according to historian Daniel Pipes. "They provided labor, engaged in commerce, sold land, sold arms, handed over state assets, provided intelligence about enemy forces, spread rumors and dissension, convinced fellow Palestinians to surrender, fought the Yishuv's enemies, and even operated behind enemy lines." He added: "Israel would not have come into being without the help of cooperative Palestinians."[11]

Unfortunately, their leaders were assassinated by the Grand Mufti of Jerusalem, Mohammed Amin al-Husseini, who was allied with the Nazis. In 1940, when the Holocaust was underway, the Mufti asked the Nazis to acknowledge the Arab right "to settle the question of Jewish elements in Palestine and other Arab countries . . . along lines similar to those used to solve the Jewish question in Germany."[12]

But the Mufti's followers in Palestine were not threatened by Jewish immigrants fleeing the Holocaust and later re-establishing the State of Israel.

"Israel did not fight 'Palestinians' for independence, but Jordanians, Egyptians, Iraqis, Lebanese, and Syrians" who were invading the new state in 1948, writes Ron Cantor, president of Shelanu, the Messianic Jewish television station in Israel. "The Jews have an unbroken link and presence to the Land going back more than 3,000 years. . . The term 'Palestinian' always referred

10. Cohen, *Army of Shadows*
11. Pipes
12. Peters, *From Time Immemorial,* 37

to any inhabitant of the region regardless of ethnicity. Jews were considered Palestinian." [13]

The Jewish exiles returning to Palestine didn't displace those Arab residents who were still living there after the Ottoman Empire collapsed following the First World War.

"The Jews did not fight against the Ottoman occupier but joined their community," Cantor continues, just as arriving Arabs were doing up to 1948. "They bought property. Created farms. Strengthened the economic outlook (which was bleak before they arrived) and created jobs. Fact: the ancestors of more than half of those who call themselves Palestinians today arrived after the Jews began to redeem the land in the late 1800s because of the economic opportunities. They came from all over the Middle East."[14]

On the eve of Israel's War of Independence, the Jewish Haifa Workers Council issued an appeal to Arab residents of Haifa not to flee: "For years we have lived together in our city. Do not fear. . . Do not bring upon yourself tragedy by unnecessary evacuation. . . In this city, yours and ours, Haifa, the gates are open for work, for life, and for peace for you and your families." [15]

On April 26, 1948, the District Police Headquarters in Haifa reported: "An appeal has been made to the Arabs by the Jews to re-open their shops and businesses in order to relieve the difficulties of feeding the Arab population." Nevertheless, "Arab leaders reiterated their determination to evacuate the entire Arab population."

Thousands of these Arab residents returned to their native Lebanon. After the war, they turned down invitations to return to Haifa. They had never been long-term Palestinian residents. And they did not leave by force. Even the Arab-sponsored Institute for Palestine Studies in Beirut acknowledged that 68 percent of Arab refugees in 1948 left without seeing an Israeli soldier.[16]

After Israel's War of Independence, only 156,000 Arabs (out of 700,000) remained in the resurrected State of Israel. So many

---

13. Ron Cantor, "The War Over Jewish History"

14. Ron Cantor, "The War Over Jewish History"

15. Peters, *From Time Immemorial,* 13

16. Peters, *From Time Immemorial.* 13–14

Arabs had voluntarily fled that the Jordanian daily newspaper *Al-Urdunn* wrote on April 1953 that Arab leaders had been responsible for their flight. During a meeting of the UN Special Political Committee on March 11, 2019, Israeli representative David Ramin argued that in 1948 they had spread false rumors about Israeli atrocities in order to instill terror in the hearts of the Arabs in Palestine until they had fled, leaving their homes and property to the enemy. With regard to those displaced in 1967, after the Six Day War, he pointed out that Israel had permitted 72,000 to return to their homes.[17]

And to this day the Arab world has treated them as refugees, with only Jordan, and to some extent Lebanon, granting them citizenship.

As for the original designation of the Holy Land as "Palestine," historian Michael Zimmerman writes that the Roman Emperor Hadrian spitefully renamed the region after the Israelis' ancient enemies, the Philistines:

"He renamed Judea with a word from distant history— 'Palestina' . . . for the Philistines, who were invaders from the sea when the Hebrews were returning from slavery in Egypt. . . The people called Philistines of the biblical period disappeared from history more than seven centuries before the decree of the Roman emperor Hadrian.

"Ironically, with British resuscitation of the name Palestine in the late nineteenth century, the first modern people who called themselves Palestinians were Jews of early modern Zionism in the late 1800s . . . Local Arabs of the area before the 1960s commonly referred to themselves as Arabs, Syrians or Bedouin. In those days, the term 'Palestinian' referred to the Jews in the land. . ."[18]

Now, will Palestinian Arabs ever accept Palestinian Jews in the Holy Land, so that a Jewish state and an Arab state can live side by side? Three times the Israelis have offered a Palestinian state in the West Bank and Gaza and part of the Old City of Jerusalem: At Camp David in 2000, at Taba in 2001, and in Jerusalem in 2008.

17. "Report of UN Special Political Committee"
18. Zimmerman, "Battir: A Palestinian Village"

The Arab negotiators walked away each time. Signing a final peace agreement ending the conflict for all time would require them to recognize a Jewish state in western Palestine.

As Israel's legendary statesman Abba Eban famously often quipped, the Palestinian Arab leaders never miss an opportunity to miss an opportunity to make peace.

Hamas has never joined the Palestinian Authority and Fatah, the PLO's main guerrilla group, in peace negotiations with Israel, insisting that a Jewish state must never be allowed in Palestine. This raises the question: If a Palestinian Arab state were carved out of the West Bank, wouldn't Gaza remain a stateless terrorist entity? Hamas has held power there since 2006 and refuses to hold new elections.

Nor is there any chance of reconciliation between the rulers of Gaza and the West Bank. Five months after the Hamas attack, Fatah condemned Hamas as "those who were responsible for the return of the occupation to the Gaza Strip [by the IDF] and [who] caused the Nakba [catastrophe] which our people live."[19]

Even with the two-state solution on life support (the "West Bank" hopelessly "Judaized"), we still hear people reciting the old mantra that peace will come to the Middle East once we have an independent Palestinian state in Judea and Samaria. What sort of magic wand do they have? Didn't they see what happened after Israel unilaterally withdrew from Gaza in 2005? Don't they care about the fate of millions of Israeli Jewish civilians and their children if the West Bank becomes another Gaza? The world's first Palestinian state will be born as a terrorist state.

And that is why the Israel Defense Forces had been cracking down on terrorists in the West Bank a year before Benjamin Netanyahu returned to power in late 2022 and formed the most extreme right-wing government in Israel's history. In fact, Hamas had been infiltrating the West Bank, seeking to supplant the Palestinian Authority, which it had violently kicked out of Gaza in 2007.

As a journalist who has frequently visited the Middle East, I have many Jewish friends in Israel, but I also have warm relations

---

19. Frantzman, "Tensions Between Hamas and Fatah," 12

with many Palestinian Arabs in Jerusalem. My wife Shirah and I know the family that runs Munir's falafel stand inside Jaffa Gate in the Old City. Whenever we're there, they invite us into their kitchen for a free lunch. Upstairs from Munir's is the office of another longtime Arab friend, architect and engineer Ismael Obaydat. He's a peace activist, and every year, when Arab shops close in protest of Jerusalem Day, he marches with the Jewish throng through the Old City and down to the Western Wall.

Back home in Buffalo, I wrote an award-winning article in the *Buffalo News'* Sunday magazine in 1983 about local Palestinian Arabs longing to return to Palestine someday. (See Chapter 7, "No Place to Call Their Own.")

In 1985, I was in Jordan, interviewing Palestinian Arab refugees about "land-for-peace" for the *Buffalo News* (and for the *Jerusalem Post,* which couldn't get a reporter into the country because they were still technically at war). Most of the refugees told me they favored Arafat's offer of peace with Israel in return for Gaza and the West Bank. *But I also learned that nine out of every ten refugee families were originally from what is now Israel, and that is where they want to return. "Land-for-peace" was doomed to failure from the very beginning.* The series that I wrote for the *Buffalo News* won an award from the Society of Professional Journalists.[20]

Palestinian Arabs claim that Jewish immigrants from post-Holocaust Europe came and took their land in 1948, when the State of Israel was resurrected. However, the new state occupied only the half of western Palestine that had been assigned to Jews by the United Nations partition plan of 1947. Jewish leaders had accepted the plan but it was rejected by the Grand Mufti of Jerusalem.

The State of Israel was resurrected in 1948 and survived, despite attacks by several Arab nations. If the Arabs had accepted Israel's independence, the Palestinian Arabs would today be controlling Gaza, the West Bank and most of Jerusalem.

What happened to the land that the UN had reserved for Arabs? Egypt quickly occupied Gaza, and Jordan took over the West Bank, and for the next 19 years neither nation ever tried to create

20. Cardinale, "Encounters in Jordan," 5

a Palestinian state. (In fact, when Israel made peace with Egypt in 1979 by returning the Sinai desert captured in 1967, the Egyptians refused to take back Gaza as well, with its teeming and restless Palestinian Arab population.)

When the PLO was born in 1964, its goal was to "liberate Palestine." But all that was left for the PLO to "liberate" was the land assigned by the UN to the Jews in 1947.

My heart goes out to Palestinian Arab refugees, the world's latest victims of war. As for the morality of Israel's "occupying" the West Bank after recovering it in a defensive war in 1967, this has always been the rule of the jungle throughout human history. There are winners and losers. Nobody gives away newly captured land (except Israel, which voluntarily returned the Sinai to Egypt, and forcefully evacuated Jews from Gaza).

The world refers to Judea and Samaria as the "occupied Palestinian territories." Why? Because that is where Syrians, Lebanese, Egyptians and other Arabs fled as war refugees after having lived in western Palestine *for varying numbers of years.* The question is: How long had any of them been living in Palestine to call themselves Palestinians? No great numbers were living in Palestine while it languished as a neglected district of the Ottoman Empire.

Furthermore, this is not the first time these lands were conquered and "occupied." All of Palestine was occupied by the Romans, who destroyed the Temple and expelled the Jews 2,000 years ago. Earlier, from 724 to 721 BC, Samaria was occupied by the Assyrians, who deported 27,290 residents, most of them Jewish, and replaced them with captives from other regions (who came to be known as Samaritans).[21]

Both Jews and Arab Muslims claim to have spiritual roots in the Holy Land. Those who dismiss Israel's biblical claim to its ancestral homeland should also dismiss the religious claims of Muslims to the land: Nowhere in the Quran did Mohammad even mention the existence of Jerusalem. The golden Dome of the Rock was built between 685 and 691—decades after his death in 632. I've been inside this shrine, and I have felt the impression of

21. "Were All the Israelites Deported?"

a man's foot—in a hard surface concealed under cloth—supposedly made when Mohammad mounted his horse for his visit to heaven. So how could he have mounted his horse in Jerusalem half a century after he died?

The invisible impression feels like it was made in wet cement. Even if it is a rock, some may argue that it was there for years before the shrine was built around it. But no such rock was on Mount Moriah in the time of King David, who purchased it as a *flat* threshing floor from Araunah for 50 shekels (2 Sam 24:24). Nor does the Old Testament refer to it when telling the story of how Abraham was ready to sacrifice his son Isaac (or Ishmael, according to the Quran) there. So, where did this rock come from? And when was it placed there?

Moreover, the Ottoman Turks showed no Muslim veneration for Palestine during their four centuries of rule, shamefully neglecting it. When Mark Twain visited in 1867 he found it "desolate and unlovely . . . a hopeless, dreary, heartbroken land," adding: "There was hardly a tree or a shrub anywhere. Even the olive and the cactus, those fast friends of a worthless soil, had almost deserted the country."[22]

Only the Palestinian Jews who returned during the 1900s cared enough about Palestine to make the desert bloom, after the region had been neglected under the Ottoman Turks from 1517 to 1917. Palestinian Arab commentators have attempted to deride this claim as erasure of their history and claim that *they* had made the desert bloom before the Jews arrived. But they have been forced to acknowledge that the arriving Jews had what the Arabs lacked—capital, expertise, technology and their socialist kibbutz communal system of shared labor.

How could anyone believe that the post-Holocaust Jews were attracted to the Holy Land because the Arabs still living there had made (or even were making) the desert bloom?

It was the Jews who fulfilled the biblical prophecy, "The wilderness and the wasteland shall be glad for them, and the desert

22. Twain, *The Innocents Abroad*, 607

shall rejoice and blossom as the rose; it shall blossom abundantly and rejoice, even with joy and singing." (Is 35:12)

And now the leaders of Israel are activating their full inheritance as Palestinian Jews. The excesses that we are seeing have prompted me to coin a term for what was coming: The Palestinian Jewish Revolt. In all fairness, Benjamin Netanyahu's ultra-religious partners are justly concerned with the secularization of Israeli society, to the point where Tel Aviv has become a major tourist destination for gays. Roughly 200,000 Israeli Jews attend its annual "gay pride" parade.

"He gave them the lands of the Gentiles," according to Psalm 105:44–45, "that they might observe His statutes and keep His laws." They lost the land and went into exile through disobedience—and can lose it again if they continue to try God's forbearance.

The Jewish state was resurrected in 1948 by mostly secular Jews. David Ben-Gurion, Israel's first prime minister, declared that "the books of the Bible declare the glory of Israel"—not of God—for "the Bible is our own creation." But the Orthodox saw 1948 as their "return to Zion" (Ps 126:1) and they made the Hebrew Scriptures the centerpiece of their school curriculum. Their return after the Holocaust confirmed the faithfulness of the God of Israel and legitimized Zionism.

However, the *secular Zionism* of today's non-Orthodox Jews poses a serious threat to the Jewish state remaining authentically Jewish. The Bible has been marginalized in the school curriculum (indeed, even Holocaust studies have given way to lessons on the plight of the Palestinian Arab refugees). The guardian of Israel (Ps 121:4) is no longer God but the Israel Defense Forces.

But now the IDF found itself engulfed in a war that only God could win.

4

Zionism Goes Ultra-Religious

THE XENOPHOBIC, ULTRA-NATIONALIST MOVEMENT that has be-witched the Western World has now sprung up in full bloom in Israel, as settlers in the West Bank (Judea and Samaria) step up their "price tag" violence against Palestinian Arabs with little or no opposition by the IDF or by the Israeli government elected in late 2022 with settlers' support.

After making a political comeback in late 2022, Benjamin Netanyahu—elected prime minister for the sixth nonconsecutive time—was unable to form a coalition because he was on trial on several serious charges of corruption.

Unwilling to step aside as the head of his Likud party (and perhaps allow a Likud puppet to take the title of prime minister), Netanyahu was left with only the most extreme right-wing religious parties to form a governing coalition.

This was the shocking outcome after Israeli voters, for the fifth time since 2019, went to the polls in attempts to break the political deadlock that had paralyzed the country for three and a half years. Each of those elections was, in effect, a referendum on Netanyahu, who refused to step aside for the good of the nation.

Under the new ruling parties, settlers had even freer rein to commit "price tag" violence against Arabs in retaliation for the Supreme Court's rulings in favor of Arabs who sued over discrimination.

Netanyahu assembled the most extreme right-wing government in the nation's history. And none of the parties was likely to bolt from the coalition, because this was their once-in-a-lifetime opportunity to reverse the secularist trend and give birth to a truly religious State of Israel. Thirty-two of the coalition's 64 members in the 120-seat Knesset were with religious parties, leading to outcries of "theocracy!" from the opposition, which supports such liberal, non-Jewish practices as homosexuality and unrestricted abortion.

"For them, the State of Israel is at best an instrument creating conditions for the Messiah's coming," wrote Leslie Susser in *Jerusalem Report*. "At worst, in its secularism and liberal democracy, it is an impediment. For all [radical party leaders] the coming of the Messiah is the supreme goal."[1]

No doubt Benjamin Netanyahu had been emboldened back in 2017 by the Trump administration's proposed peace plan, called by its proponents the "deal of the century." (Palestinian Authority President Mahmoud Abbas immediately called it the "slap of the century.") Like Netanyahu, Donald Trump was struggling to return to power in hopes of influencing federal prosecutors to curtail his criminal prosecutions. And Bibi—who is not Orthodox—Trump—who is not religious—both allied themselves with some of their most radical religious voters in order to cling to power at all costs.

There are other striking similarities. Their 1930s fascist predecessors had their own violent militias—Mussolini's "Blackshirts" and Hitler's "Brownshirts." Trump had the Proud Boys and other insurrectionists attacking the Capitol on January 6, 2021, and Netanyahu gave violent settlers more freedom to attack Arab communities in the West Bank. And like the fascists of old, both leaders have exploited divisions in society and scapegoated minorities (Arabs in Israel, and illegal immigrants entering the United States).

1. Susser, "Democracy Under Threat," 20

Even the Republican Party has gone that dangerous route. At the time of Netanyahu's return to power, U.S. Congressman Kevin McCarthy had become speaker of the House by selling himself to a handful of ultra-right Republicans called the House Freedom Caucus—who then demanded that he hold America's credit rating hostage by refusing to raise the debt limit unless drastic cuts in spending were approved by President Joseph Biden.

Likewise, Netanyahu had sold himself to radical religious coalition partners—who demanded legislation to curb the Supreme Court on grounds that it was dominated by secular liberal activist justices who often ruled in favor of Arab claims. Under this radical judicial reform, the Knesset would have more control over court appointments—*and could overrule a Supreme Court ruling by a simple majority vote.*

This flew in the face of Netanyahu's statement in 2012: "I believe that a strong, independent court allows for the existence of all other institutions in a democracy. . . In places with no strong and independent court system, rights cannot be protected."[2]

Outraged at this attack on democracy, hundreds of thousands of Israelis—including academics, professionals and even military reservists—demonstrated in major cities for months to stop the judicial reform, or at least to bring about a compromise. The clashing of demonstrators and counter-demonstrators prompted President Isaac Herzog to warn of a civil war in Israel. Herzog said he had heard "real, deep hatred," albeit from "a very small minority of people. . . I heard from people, from all sides, that, heaven forbid, the idea of blood in the streets no longer shocks them."[3]

On July 24, 2024, the Knesset passed a law prohibiting Israeli courts from using what's called the "reasonableness doctrine" to review decisions made by the Israeli cabinet, government ministers, and certain other elected officials. In the face of continuing protests across the land, Netanyahu put off indefinitely a law permitting the Knesset to overrule a Supreme Court ruling.

2. "Netanyahu in 2012"
3. Kampeas, "Israeli President Herzog Warns"

Forced to give key positions of power to the most rabid of his right-wing coalition partners, the prime minister saddled himself with some cabinet members who had criminal records for violence against Palestinian Arabs and who seemed intent on provoking them to rise up with a third intifada. These three right-wing party leaders stood out in the incoming Netanyahu government:

Itmar Ben-Gvir (leader of the far-right Jewish Power party) was convicted in 2007 of racist incitement against Arabs by supporting an anti-Arab group that Israel and the U.S. classify as a terrorist organization. Ben-Gvir called Arab members of the Knesset "a fifth column," or enemy within, and said Arabs should be expelled from Israel. (About 20 percent of Israel's population are Arabs with Israeli citizenship.)

Israel's most polarizing far-right politician, Ben-Gvir became Netanyahu's minister of national security overseeing the police. This put him in a position to further relax the government's resistance to settler violence against Arabs. The Police Retired Commissioners' Forum declared that Ben-Gvir posed a great danger to Israel's national security.

Back in 1993, young Ben-Gvir was among those settlers calling for the elimination of Prime Minister Yizhak Rabin for signing the Oslo Accords with Yasser Arafat, offering more land to the Arabs; Rabin was assassinated in 1995 by an ultra-nationalist Israeli. Three decades later, Ben-Gvir is among those distributing stickers that celebrate Rabin's death.

A month after the attack from Gaza, a member of his party, Heritage Minister Amichai Eliyahu, said that one of Israel's options in the war against Hamas could be to drop a nuclear bomb on the Gaza Strip.

Bezalel Smotrich (head of the Religious Zionist party) weakly attempted to claim that the judicial reform would not retroactively apply to Netanyahu and "would not impact" his trial. Netanyahu himself also insisted that if passed, the reform wouldn't affect his trial. However, if his transgressions were decriminalized by the Knesset, and the courts were unable to reverse it, his trial would not be able to continue.

A resident of Kedumim in the Israeli settlements, Smotrich was arrested in 2005 while in possession of 700 litres of gasoline, on suspicion of participating in an attempt to blow up the Ayalon Highway, a major arterial road. He was held in jail for three weeks, but not charged after refusing to speak. In 2006, he helped organize the "Beast Parade" as part of protests against a gay pride parade in Jerusalem, although he later admitted regret at the incident. He is co-founder of the NGO Regavim, which pursues legal action in the Israeli court system against constructions undertaken by Palestinians, Bedouins, and other Arabs in Israel and the West Bank without government authorization.

Aryeh Deri (head of the Shas party) was convicted back in 2000 of taking $155,000 in bribes while serving as the interior minister, and was given a three-year jail sentence. He was re-elected to the Knesset in 2013. However, Ovadia Yosef, the founder of Shas, attacked Deri, calling him a wicked man and a thief. Deri resigned, but after Rabbi Yosef's death he returned to office under Netanyahu, who appointed him both minister of interior and minister of health.

In January 2023, the Supreme Court ruled that Deri was ineligible to hold a position as a cabinet minister. "This is a person who has been convicted three times of offenses throughout his life, and he violated his duty to serve the public loyally and lawfully while serving in senior public positions," said Court President Esther Hayut. "Having Deri in charge of two of the most important ministries in the government damages the image and reputation of the country's legal system and contradicts principles of ethical conduct and legality." Shas threatened to withdraw from the co-alition and potentially bring it down if Deri was not allowed to remain in the government.[4]

∾

Sooner or later the Netanyahu government would fall, but the damage it had inflicted on Israeli democracy was not easily revers-ible. Nor was there any way to reverse the worldwide Jew-hatred that was unleashed when Bibi put the release of Israeli hostages below his priority of destroying Hamas, resulting in scores of civil-ian casualties in Gaza.

One of Bibi's cabinet members dismissed demands that he agree to a cease-fire so that hostages could be returned: Settle-ments and National Missions Minister Orit Strock was asked on Army Radio on May 8, 2024 whether her Religious Zionist party would leave the government if a deal was signed. She replied:

"You essentially say, 'I'll be satisfied with 20 or 33 hostages.' This is a reckless deal that turns its back on the goals of the war on their [hostages'] behalf. We sent out soldiers to battle, some of whom did not come back, and some of whom came back wound-ed. [Then the government] tells them: 'You know what? Drop it. We're throwing it all in the trash in order to save 20 or 33 people or who knows how many?' Such a government has absolutely no right to exist."[5]

Even the Jewish state's most loyal friends find it difficult to comprehend how the Israel Defense Forces—known for precision in minimizing collateral deaths during wartime—could be causing so many civilian deaths day after day in Gaza. While searching for some psychological insight into the matter, the following thoughts have crossed my mind:

Israelis never developed an Anglo-Saxon culture—even though they were ruled by Britain under its Palestinian Man-date from 1918 to 1948—and even though Ashkenazi Holocaust

---

4. Tarnopolsky, "Bibi's Rogue Minister"

5. *Jerusalem Post* Staff, "We Have No Right," 4

survivors came from Europe, particularly Germany. Rather, they have what I would call a Mediterranean culture, particularly because of their Sephardic newcomers from north Africa, who now outnumber Ashkenazi Jews. Thus, Israelis never embraced the restraint and "stiff upper lip" common to British and even most white Americans. Emotionally, they have more in common with Italians and Spanish than with the British and Germans.

Then there is the Israelis' fast-paced lifestyle. Lunch is supposedly 30 minutes but I have seen Israelis eating an apple or a piece of cheese as their lunch, while remaining on the job. If the Jews' frenzied work week weren't shut down for 24 hours for Shabbat, I believe the national burnout would be staggering.

Israelis are intense survivors, in matters large and small. I recall one day when an elderly Israeli woman (possibly a Holocaust survivor) stepped on my foot to get ahead of me in line! I just smiled.

Israelis are also impulsive. Many bureaucrats and store clerks have hung up the phone on me when they lost their patience with this American tourist. Impulsiveness seems to be a tribal trait. The Apostle Peter cut off the right ear of the high priest's servant at the time of Jesus' arrest in Gethsemane. Jesus healed the ear and told him, "Put your sword back into its place, for all those who take the sword will perish by the sword." (Mt 2:52) This verse is speaking about self-willed aggression outside the bounds of the law—not self-defense. Now think of the IDF . . .

I once drove a rented car from Tiberius all the way up the mountain to ancient Safed, and I'll never do it again. Even riding in a van from the airport near Tel Aviv to Jerusalem is an adventure I always dread. After leaving the highway, the *sherut* drivers will carelessly barrel through a neighborhood, eager to arrive and take up their next fare. In 2022, Israel had a road mortality rate of 3.6 deaths per 100,000 people, with pedestrians accounting for 31 percent of all road deaths.

In addition, Israelis have endured six (now seven) existentialist wars since 1948, and their families have experienced death and permanent disablement in defense of their country. They have lost more than 25,000 soldiers in wars. In America, it would have amounted to 850,000 war deaths. It has hardened recent generations of soldiers. This is the fifth war with Hamas—and if Hamas is ever to be eliminated, with no more periodic "mowing the lawn," it's now or never.

None of this can justify those civilian casualties. But what might explain this tragedy is how Hamas in effect lured Israel into Gaza after years of digging hundreds of miles of tunnels as an underground fortress and hiding place virtually impossible to penetrate without ferocious—and sometimes reckless—bombing in the fog of war. Think of the IDF's accidental killing of several civilian workers by bombing World Central Kitchen trucks misidentified as terrorist vehicles on April 1, 2024.

The following month, on May 26, an Israeli airstrike killed at least 45 people when it hit tents for displaced people in Rafah, after Hamas fired eight rockets from near two mosques targeting central Israel for the first time in months. The IDF said it targeted a Hamas compound and killed two senior Hamas leaders—Yassin Rabia, a senior Hamas commander leading the terrorist group's operations in the West Bank, and Khaled Nagar, a senior official in Hamas' West Bank command. Both terrorists had been serving life sentences in Israeli prison but were freed in 2011 as part of a prisoner swap deal for the release of IDF soldier Gilad Shalit.

The IDF said about 70 investigations had been launched, thus far, into incidents that raised suspicion of criminal offenses. Meanwhile, the International Court of Justice ordered Israel to immediately halt its military operation in Rafah, but it had no enforcement power.

To make matters worse, Netanyahu long refused to consider a long humanitarian cease-fire, not only because it would give Hamas time to recover, but because it would cause his most radical coalition partners to leave the government. Moreover, if a cease-fire were to result in the release of the remaining hostages and a final cessation of military action in Gaza, Israel would no longer be at war—opening the way for new elections, which he would almost certainly lose.

Nor did the government have a plan for "the day after" the war—who would rule Gaza? The prime minister long refused to hold cabinet discussions on this because his far-right partners might bolt his coalition. In fact, they have called for permanent occupation, "voluntary emigration" of large numbers of Arabs to countries that would receive them, and rebuilding of Jewish settlements in Gaza.

Hamas proposed a phased agreement in which it would release all of the hostages in return for hundreds of Arab prisoners, Israel would agree to a long cease-fire and withdraw all of its forces. Although that would leave Hamas in control of Gaza and allow it to rebuild its military, thousands of Israelis took to the streets in the spring of 2024 demanding that Israel take such a deal, as the only way to get the hostages back.

A quick end to the war would leave Bibi without the protections of his office as his trials continued in three corruption cases. And he might never get the Knesset to legalize the actions that brought about those charges. In Case 1000, he is charged with receiving gifts from billionaire benefactors. Case 2000 charges him with negotiating to receive positive coverage in an unfriendly newspaper in exchange for curtailing its competitors. In Case 4000, he is charged with bribery, fraud and breach of trust in granting regulatory benefits to a telecom giant in exchange for good publicity in that company's news outlet.

In the end, Gaza would probably be Netanyahu's downfall, just as it was for Prime Minister Ariel Sharon, who suddenly suffered a debilitating stroke after unilaterally turning over Gaza to the Arabs in 2005.

❧

Here is a summary of what this far-right coalition did during its first several months of governing to so provoke Israeli citizens—and also to provoke Palestinian Arabs to fight back:

— In February 2023, scores of Israeli settlers went on a violent rampage in the town of Huwara in the northern West Bank,

46

setting homes and dozens of cars on fire after two settlers were killed by an Arab gunman. The IDF did nothing to stop the settlers' violence, standing by as emergency vehicles were blocked from reaching the scene. Some soldiers fired stun grenades and teargas at the Arabs, who retaliated by throwing stones at the rioting settlers.

— The IDF intensified its incursions into Arab communities in the West Bank in search of terrorists. Most of these encounters resulted in gun battles, leaving Arabs killed or wounded. These escalated to the point that, on the night of May 22, 2023, some 200 soldiers and 70 military vehicles took part in an attack in the Balata refugee camp in Nablus, killing three terrorists and wounding three others.

— National Security Minister Ben Gvir visited the Temple Mount, declaring "We are in charge!" Even more provocative was the march in the Arab neighborhood of the Old City on Jerusalem Day, poking in their faces the Israel victory in 1967. Many marchers chanted racist slogans and assaulted Arabs.

— In April, tens of thousands of Netanyahu supporters demonstrated in favor of the judicial reform, and soon Israelis on both sides were clashing in the streets.

— On June 21, after the murder of four Israelis in the West Bank settlement of Eli, the Netanyahu government announced: "Our response to terror is to hit it hard and build on our land," and it authorized 1,000 new homes for Eli.

— Also in June, Defense Minister Yoav Gallant warned that "we may be required to fulfill our duty in order to protect the integrity of Israel" by attacking Iran, which now had enough enriched uranium to produce two nuclear bombs.[6]

Bible-believing Christians might ask themselves: If the government becomes emboldened to extend its Palestinian Jewish Revolt to the international level, could the resulting

6. Magid. "Gallant Warns Israel"

chaos hasten the final days? Might this be what will prompt the Antichrist to marshal the seven-year peace treaty between Israel and her enemies, as prophesied in the Book of Revelation (based on the Book of Daniel)?

Meanwhile, Israeli Messianic Jews, who believe in Jesus, have also become a target of the Netanyahu administration, as its provocative policies have emboldened the Orthodox to physically attack them. Ron Cantor of Shelanu, the Christian television station in Israel, sent me an email in June that his wife, Elana, had been seriously injured while praying at the Western Wall during a three-week prayer event by Messianic Jews.

"The deputy mayor of Jerusalem, Aryeh King, called for Orthodox Jews to come protest the event," he said. "Elana was pushed and punched as she entered the venue. She was struck in a crowd of militant, angry men for more than five minutes. She was wearing sandals, and they stomped on her feet. Finally a tour guide and a police officer rescued her."

Elana suffered a serious neck injury. The Cantors went to the police. "The woman who interviewed her was a Haredi (ultra-Orthodox) and she said to Elana, 'Thank you so much for coming in and filing a complaint. People need to know that these extremists do not represent us.'"

The incident was condemned by members of the Knesset, and Speaker Amir Ohana "made it clear that Israel sees Christians as friends."[7]

"During the attack, I saw Yeshua next to me," Elana added on September 20 in a followup email to me and others. "I wouldn't trade this nearness for anything in the world." She added this request to believers in America: "Please be in prayer for my beloved Israel. My nation is in turmoil [and] is being torn up right now. I don't know how much more we can take."[8]

---

7. Ron Cantor, email to author
8. Elana Cantor, email to author

— By July 2023, increasing Arab resistance to the IDF's incursions into Jenin prompted the military to begin a major operation like none seen in the West Bank in decades. A longtime hotbed of terrorist activities, Jenin had been the scene of 50 shooting attacks in the previous six months. IDF drones and aircraft struck targets and a large number of ground troops entered the city. Armored bulldozers entered to clear roadways and identify and avoid improvised explosive devices. Heavy gunfights broke out between the IDF and terrorists firing from houses and mosques. One of 19 refugee camps in the West Bank, the Jenin refugee camp (housing about 20,000) had been turned into a fortress as IDF forces intensified their search for terrorists in the city of Jenin. The terrorists had set up metal barriers and obstacles to vehicles and had hidden large explosive charges on the roads the IDF was expected to use. During the two-day operation, a dozen Arab terrorists were killed and six explosives factories were dismantled.

Jenin was a turning point. The fire that had been sparked by the radicals in Netanyahu's coalition now threatened to spiral out of control and ignite a bona fide civil war in the Holy Land.

Israel was not to blame for stepping up its searches for terrorists in Jenin. The Palestinian Authority, which exercises limited police power in the West Bank, had more and more neglected its responsibility to assist the IDF in keeping the peace. Weak and corrupt, the PA neglected its own Arabs, resulting in more crime and Arab-on-Arab murders—as well as the rise of independent terrorist groups of mostly young men who seek to take matters into their own hands. For years, the PA has seemed on the verge of collapse, which would further complicate the IDF's job of establishing security in the West Bank.

The IDF's valid response unfortunately resulted in this rising cycle of violence. The critical problem now, however, was that Netanyahu's extremist partners seemed eager to see a monumental confrontation break out, giving them an excuse to begin expelling thousands of Arabs from the West Bank—which they have long wanted to annex to Israel.

— By September 2023, opposition leader Yair Lapid declared: "The prime minister has lost control of his ministers. Each of them pursues their own dangerous policy. . . We are approaching a violent, multi-front confrontation. What is even more dangerous is that the government is not coordinated with the security establishment."[9]

Nor was the security establishment aware of the months-long plot by Hamas to attack Israel on October 7—a Sabbath day and during Simchat Torah—on the fiftieth anniversary of the Yom Kippur War, which it had also failed to see coming.

By 2024, after several weeks of war, Netanyahu's popularity had plummeted amid calls for his resignation. He resisted persistent calls to pause the IDF's actions in Gaza—to admit humanitarian aid and to arrange hostage and prisoner exchanges. But he had another reason to avoid a cease-fire— that the longer the country was at war, the longer he could cling to power and not face an election. He could probably never again be elected to office, so now it was a matter of restoring his legacy as the leader who destroyed Hamas.

Meanwhile, the Israeli hostages still held in Gaza were a secondary priority of Netanyahu to destroying Hames . . . and may have been virtually written off as future martyrs for the Jewish state's survival.

~

Many years ago, my Palestinian Arab friend Marwan Khatib predicted that someday the Israelis would decimate their country in a civil war, opening the door for a State of Palestine to replace Israel. In those days the only inkling of an imminent civil war was the

9. Keller-Lynn, "Lapid: Netanyahu Has 'Lost Control'"

possibility that Jewish settlers would fight the IDF and refuse to leave the West Bank under some future peace agreement.

From a Christian evangelical standpoint, an all-out conflict with Arabs in the West Bank and Gaza might create an evil opportunity to expel Arabs from those "occupied territories." This might provoke a regional war that might hasten the coming of the Messiah, who would defeat Israel's enemies and begin a millennium of justice and peace.

On a more down-to-earth note, Netanyahu's opponents charged that his long-term goal during all these election years was to assemble a Knesset that would decriminalize his actions that had resulted in his three indictments. His most pragmatic supporters no doubt would cite Torah law as superior to civil law, as taught by their late mentor, Rabbi Meir Kahane (see next chapter).

The mood of this religious coalition might be summed up with: "Enough already about the 'poor downtrodden Palestinians' sharing our homeland—what about the Palestinian Jews who resurrected this country after two millennia of dispersion and persecution?"

Long resentful that Israel had been resurrected by secular, socialist Jews, the Orthodox finally found themselves in a position to assert themselves as the Palestinian Jews. In 2018 the Knesset passed the "Basic Law: Israel as the Nation-State of the Jewish People," informally known as the Nation-State Bill or the Nationality Bill. It specifies the nature of Israel as the nation-state of the Jewish people. It was met with sharp criticism internationally and was branded as racist and undemocratic by some critics.

However, the Bible says nothing about democracy as a system for ruling Israel. Historically, minorities were always present in the Land of Israel—and often benefited from the biblical command to deal justly with "the stranger in your midst"—but of course they were never given a voice in government.

And so, what I call this Palestinian Jewish Revolt has posed a historic challenge to democracy (which some would call a non-biblical and "un-Jewish" form of government). Only time would tell how far it would go. Even if Netanyahu's coalition failed to achieve its ultimate goal, the dangerous precedent he had set would keep the door open to a future government's assault on democracy and on the original Zionist dream of peaceful coexistence with Arabs in the Jewish homeland.

5

The Legacy of Rabbi Meir Kahane

RABBI MEIR KAHANE AND his followers once wanted to tear down the Muslim Dome of the Rock in Jerusalem and rebuild the Temple on its original foundations. To do this, they would need the ashes of a red heifer, to purify the Jews so that they wouldn't desecrate the Holy of Holies on the Temple Mount. That's where the *Shekinah*—the Divine Presence of God—had once dwelled.

But Rabbi Kahane seldom mentioned the red heifer during the early years of his campaign to turn Israel into a more religious Jewish state. At the time that I was covering his speeches for the *Buffalo News,* his major theme was that Israel's Jewish character could only be preserved by moving the Arab residents from the "occupied territories" to other countries—mainly to neighboring Jordan, where Palestinian Arabs were already in the majority.

This made him a lightening rod for Arab protesters wherever he spoke. One night in 1981, at Buffalo State College, Rabbi Kahane had spoken for only twenty minutes when his body guards from the Jewish Defense League almost came to blows with protesting Palestinian Arab students.

"Long live Palestine!" chanted the Arab students.

"There *is* no 'Palestine'!" the bearded rabbi shouted back at them, insisting that Palestine was never a country or a people, only a regional term assigned by the Romans after exiling the Jews.

53

"Long live Palestine!" they chanted.

As the Arabs and the JDL men lunged for each other, security guards whisked Kahane out of the building and into the night. His last words were, "There *is* no 'Palestine'!"

Six months later, the scrappy little rabbi returned to Buffalo State College, mounted the stage and began: "As I was saying, there *is* no 'Palestine'!" More than 120 students clamored in the student union this night, but this time he finished his speech.

Rabbi Kahane's Kach Party in Israel called for removing Palestinian Arabs from the "occupied territories" of the West Bank (which he called by its biblical name, Judea and Samaria) and from Gaza, either by force or by paying Arab families restitution for their property. This would allow Israel to settle Jewish families on those lands, which had been promised to Israel by God.

"For God will give salvation to Zion and build the cities of Judah," the Psalmist prophesied. "They shall abide there and shall take possession of it once more." (Ps 69:35)

As for the nearly two million Arab citizens of Israel whose families had never left in 1948, Kahane said they could remain in Israel proper. But they should be stripped of their voting rights in national elections, so that their swelling population could never take over the democratic government and turn Israel into a non-Jewish state.

Arabs already have a Palestinian state, one that should have been named *Palestine* when it was created in 1947, according to Kahane. That country is Jordan, which occupies all of traditional eastern Palestine. (Israel was left with less than half of western Palestine when it gained independence a year later, in 1948.) About 70 percent of Jordan's citizens are Palestinian Arabs, whose families fled western Palestine in 1948 and 1967.

Some 700,000 Arabs fled western Palestine when Israel declared its independence in May 1948 and the neighboring Arab countries attacked the Jewish state. Many of the Arab residents were driven out by Jewish fighters, but many others left voluntarily—with the encouragement of the Arab world—thinking they could return when the Jews had been defeated. But that wasn't the outcome.

Of all the Arab countries that rejected the two-state solution and invaded the land, only Jordan immediately offered citizenship to fleeing Palestinian Arabs. Yet even today, many Palestinian Arabs still live in refugee camps in Jordan and have limited opportunities in the government.

The other Arab nations that attacked Israel have refused to welcome Palestinian Arab refugees, preferring to use them as pawns against Israel. Meanwhile, about 700,000 Jews fled to Israel, forced from their longtime homes in Arab countries after the foundation of Israel in 1948. The Arab world, comprising 22 countries, never forgave the Jews for forming their own tiny state in the Middle East.

In 1964 the Arab League established the Palestine Liberation Organization, and Yasser Arafat later became its president. At no time did Arafat or the PLO pressure Egypt or Jordan to establish a Palestinian state next to Israel. Rather, its goal was to eliminate the Jewish state by terrorism and "liberate" all of western Palestine for the Arabs.

Then, in June 1967, Egypt, Jordan, Syria and Lebanon amassed their armies on the borders of Israel and prepared to attack and "liberate" all the rest of western Palestine for the Arab refugees. Facing 250,000 enemy troops and 2,000 tanks on its borders, Israel struck first and not only pushed back the Arab armies but "liberated" the West Bank from Jordan, Gaza and the Sinai Desert from Egypt, and the Golan Heights from Syria. Israel then annexed the Old City of Jerusalem as its capital, which it had been in the days of King David.

After Anwar Sadat's visit in 1977, Israel returned the Sinai to Egypt in exchange for peace. And Israel evacuated Gaza and turned it over to Palestinian control in 2005.

None of the territory occupied by Israel after the Six Day War was taken from the Palestinian Arab. Except for Jerusalem, all of it was land that should have been part of a Jewish state—according to the UN's 1947 partition plan—but instead had been taken by Jordan and Egypt in 1948.

"We do not see it as an occupied territory," said Justice Elyakim Rubenstein of the Israeli Supreme Court, "because there was no recognized sovereignty there before 1948."[1]

And now, for the first time in nearly 2,000 years, Israel again had control over all of western Palestine, including the Old City of Jerusalem, which was reunited with modern-day Jerusalem as the capital of Israel—the site of the ancient (and to-be-rebuilt) Temple.

Since then, Israel has established more than 150 Jewish settlements on the West Bank, housing nearly 300,000 Jews. And the Arabs, who number more than a million on the West Bank, have added 260 settlements since 1967. The lingering question is how to grant a measure of local autonomy to Arab communities on the West Bank without creating a sovereign Palestinian state that still refuses to accept the existence of Israel.

In later years the Arab nations that had rejected the UN's partition plan of 1947 turned around and began to promote a new "two-state solution." One state, to be named Palestine, would take over the "occupied territories" and become entirely Arabic—in other words, *Judenrein*. The other state, known until now as Israel, would grant millions of Arab Palestinians the Right of Return, which would gradually transform it into an Arab-dominated state. The two states would eventually merge as Palestine, where some Jews would be permitted to live as a minority under Muslim rule, until the end of time.

Meir Kahane was back in Buffalo, New York, in 1982 on a national speaking tour while running for a seat in the Knesset, the parliament of Israel. After speaking at an Orthodox synagogue, Kahane went to the home of his host, Eric Mahr, who headed Kahane's Jewish Defense League in Buffalo.

Here, the rabbi agreed to be interviewed by me with my tape recorder. In contrast to his bombastic speeches, Kahane now spoke softly, intimately, at times almost inaudibly.

1. "Israel Says It Will Keep"

First, I asked Kahane whether there was ever a time in history when the Jews lived in Palestine and had no non-Jewish neighbors.

"Why, certainly," he said, "in Judea and Samaria thousands of years ago. There weren't any Arabs then."

There weren't Samaritans or other non-Jews living in Samaria?

"I don't know," he said, "but it was a Jewish state. In the days of the first Temple."

But there were foreigners living there, right?

"I would say there were foreigners living there, but they certainly were not voting citizens," Kahane said.

I asked him how the Hebrew Scriptures command the Jewish people to treat the foreigner living in their midst.

"First of all," Kahane said, "when it speaks of that, it uses the Hebrew word *ger*, which is translated as stranger, but *ger* means convert, it never means stranger. Now, obviously, someone who's not Jewish, certainly we should not oppress or persecute. But there's a tremendous gap, a gulf, between not persecuting someone and making him a citizen."

Doesn't the *Gamara Ketubot* in the Talmud say that the Jews may not cast out other people from Israel until the Messiah comes?

"It doesn't say that at all," Kahane replied. "It says on Page 110 that God gave two oaths to the Jews, and one to the nations. The two oaths to the Jews basically were that they should not rise up in force against the world nations. The oath that the nations gave was that they should not persecute the Jews while the Jews are in exile. All the rabbis say that when the nations broke their oath, of course we were free from our oaths."

Two wrongs make a right?

"It isn't a question of whether we were wrong," he said. "God certainly didn't want Jews to be placed in a position of having to go into gas chambers and not doing anything about it. So God said to the nations, 'Don't make gas chambers,' and to the Jews, 'You sit quietly.' They wanted to go to Palestine in the 1930s, and they were told to stay in Europe and die. And those who went lived."

Didn't the Jews establish Israel as a democracy in 1948, and doesn't Judaism require the Jewish state to give equal rights to non-Jews living in its borders?

Kahane replied that 'democracy' and the 'state' are secular concepts that arose long after Judaism, so they cannot take precedence over what the Torah has taught about Jews and Gentiles living together over the centuries. He was upset over all the secular Jews who have, in effect, adopted democracy as their religion.

"The Jews are the last of the ancient Hebrews," Kahane said. "Many Jews today—including Orthodox Jews—are assimilated Jews. They have assimilated non-Jewish concepts. . . We have Orthodox Jews here who are influenced by Thomas Jefferson. Judaism is Judaism! And the Jewish nation faces tragedy because it doesn't want to be Jewish."

I then asked Kahane about the theory of some archaeologists that the Temple once stood either north or south of the spot now occupied by the Muslim Dome of the Rock. Is there room on the Temple Mount for both the Dome of the Rock and a future, third Jewish Temple?

"I don't need an archaeologist to tell me," Kahane angrily replied. "We know, everyone knows, that on the Temple Mount, on that area on that site, stood both holy Temples. That's the holiest site in all of Judaism. The outrage is not only that Moslems came on our holiest site and built two mosques, but that the Israeli government, in its fear and panic and lack of any kind of Jewishness and Jewish faith, is so terrified that it leaves them there and orders Jews not to pray there. I want a Moslem ban, I want the mosques removed, and I want—"

"–Isn't that World War III?" I interjected. *"Wouldn't that cause all the countries that are Islamic to rise up as one and declare a holy war against Israel?"*

Kahane said something low, inaudible, as if whispering to himself.

"Hmmm?" I asked.

Speaking ever so softly, Kahane replied: "It would bring the Messiah."[2]

2. Cardinale, "Rabbi Kahane's Apartheid Policies," 13–15

6

Jewish vs. Arab Claims to the Land

ISRAEL'S VICTORY IN THE Six Day War of June 1967 sparked religious fundamentalist revivals on three levels throughout the world:

— In Israel, the reunification of the capital city of Jerusalem for the first time in 2,000 years was seen as a sign of God's miraculous championing of the return of Jews into their ancestral homelands during the twentieth century. And it accelerated the in-gathering of Jews from all over the world and the belief among religious Jews that the time of the Messiah was near.

— In the Muslim world, the sudden, humiliating defeat of four Arab armies by the tiny Jewish state was blamed on the secularization of Muslim society. It demonstrated the urgent need to enforce *shari'a* rule in Islamic countries and to take up arms in the worldwide cause of Islam. The three-year-old Palestine Liberation Organization began to display the image of the Dome of the Rock, and began to claim a pre-eminent Islamic role for Jerusalem and the Haram al-Sharif.

— In the Christian world, and particularly among evangelicals, the Lord's restoration of Jerusalem was interpreted as a sign of the end times. As David Parsons of the International Christian Embassy in Jerusalem once told me during my visit in 1985: "I know people who fell on their knees and cried out to God when they heard that Jerusalem was back in Jewish hands. It forced Christians to rethink their views toward Israel, toward Jerusalem, toward prophecy."

But what about the Palestinian Arabs, who once again were treated as mere pawns of history?

In a strange, ironic way, the Palestinian Arabs—especially those scattered refugees outside of eastern and western Palestine—might be called "the Jews of the Arab world." Like the Jews who were scattered abroad 2,000 years ago (before there ever were Arabs in Palestine), these refugees refuse to be assimilated into other societies where they reside.

Among all the Arabic peoples who lived in the Middle East under the rule of the Turkish Ottoman Empire until the First World War, only the Palestinians have failed to achieve statehood in the modern world where nations exist as sovereign states. Their immediate neighbors—the Egyptians, the Jordanians, the Syrians and the Lebanese—all became nation states. And then came the State of Israel, in western Palestine, in 1948.

As early as the late 1800s, a spirit of nationalism was beginning to awaken among the nomadic Arabs who had been living in Palestine under Turkish Ottoman rule. At the same time, the Zionist movement was beginning to stir among Jews in eastern Europe to reclaim their ancestral homeland in Palestine.

During the First World War, Britain promised to support the establishment of an independent Arab state as a reward for Arabs who were revolting against the Ottoman Empire. But in the Balfour Declaration of 1917, Britain promised to "view with favour the establishment in Palestine of a national home for the Jewish people," adding: "Nothing shall be done which may prejudice the civil and religious rights of existing non-Jewish communities in Palestine." The "existing" communities were Arab and Bedouin; note that those *existing* Arab populations would never include Arab newcomers from other countries—who would swell the *future* Arab populations in Palestine beyond the natural increase by childbirth.[1]

"Had only actual 'natural' increase taken place among the *existing* Arabs," Jane Peters writes in her book, *From Time Immemorial,* "the European and Arab-born Jews might have had their sanctuary in time to save countless Jewish lives." Instead, she said, there was a "carefully disguised Arab population increase by in-migration and illegal immigration—that matched or possibly even exceeded the Jews' immigration into their 'Jewish National Home.'"[2]

After the First World War, the victorious nations granted Britain a mandate to govern Palestine until the former Ottoman Empire's various peoples were ready for statehood. The British Mandate of Palestine originally covered the entire 48,000-plus square miles on both sides of the Jordan River. But the British broke off from Mandate Palestine all the land east of the Jordan River—two-thirds of ancient Palestine—and this became the State of Jordan in 1947. Jordan was inhabited mostly by Bedouin Muslims under their Bedouin king, and they began to be called *Jordanians*—but today 70 percent of Jordan's residents are Palestinian Arabs whose families fled from western Palestine in 1948 and 1967.

Also In 1947, the United Nations proposed a plan to partition western Palestine into two parts—one part that was already inhabited mostly by Palestinian Jews, the other past mostly by Palestinian Arabs. Although some of the Jewish families and many of the Arabic families had lived in the region for centuries, many from both groups were fairly recent immigrants. During the British occupation over Palestine, while Jewish immigrants from Europe were "illegally" entering the land (especially to escape the Holocaust), Arab immigrants from Arab countries were "illegally" entering the land as well—not only to take advantage of how the Jews were making the desert bloom, but also to counter the Jews'

---

1. Peters, *From Time Immemorial,* 217
2. Peters, *From Time Immemorial,* 337

rising numbers. A demographic race was going on for the future control of the western Palestine.

After examining the UN partition plan, the Palestinian Jews agreed, reluctantly, to accept their half of western Palestine for a future Jewish state. Unfortunately, the Palestinian Arabs never had a voice in the partition plan. Their self-appointed spokesman, the Grand Mufti of Jerusalem (who had collaborated with the Nazis during the war) rejected the UN plan, as did the neighboring Arab nations, all of them unwilling to share any part of western Palestine with a Jewish state.

The following year, in 1948, when the British pulled out of western Palestine, the Jews declared an independent State of Israel, mostly in the part designated for them under the UN partition plan. In reaction, the armies of seven Arab nations immediately invaded and attempted to crush the Jewish state. Jordanian troops occupied the West Bank, inhabited mostly by Arabs, and Egyptian troops took over Gaza, also inhabited mostly by Arabs.

Gaza and the West Bank, in fact, constituted most of the territory that the United Nations partition plan of 1947 had assigned to the Arabs. But over the next two decades, the Arab nations had done nothing to promote the establishment of a sovereign Palestinian state in those "occupied territories." Both Jordan and Egypt remained technically at war with Israel, intent on destroying it, rather than establishing a sovereign Palestinian state on the land already under their control. In fact Jordan at one point annexed the West Bank (later relinquishing any claim over it) and granted Jordanian citizenship to all of its Palestinian Arab inhabitants.

Israel was admitted as a member of the United Nations in 1949.

~

In 1964 the Palestine Liberation Organization was established by the first Arab Summit as an umbrella organization over numerous factions, including Fatah, of Yasser Arafat. Exactly what territory did it intend to *liberate*? Certainly not Egyptian-occupied Gaza or the Jordanian-occupied West Bank, before any Jewish settlements could ever have sprang up there.

If the PLO had suddenly decided to recognize the UN partition plan of 1947, it might have rightfully claimed parts of Israel that originally had been designated for Arabs on the partition map. These included central Galilee (including Nazareth), a ring around the south and west edges of the West Bank (including a corridor to Jerusalem), a northern piece of the Gaza Strip and a stretch of land south of Gaza, along the border of the Sinai. But the Palestine National Covenant called for eliminating Israel and setting up an Arab state in all of western Palestine.

In June 1967, Egypt, Jordan and Syria (aided by Iraq) amassed their armies, composed of 250,000 troops and 2,000 tanks, on Israel's borders. Their intent was to treat Israel's portion of western Palestine as if it had no sovereignty as a state—despite the UN recognition of Israel. The Arab plan was to seize all of Israel's land—or as much of it as possible—for resettlement by the approximately 700,000 Arabs who had fled from that land during the war of 1948–1949. The bulk of these refugees were living either in Jordan or the West Bank, with Jordanian citizenship; the other Arab nations had refused to absorb these refugees, preferring to take them into temporary refugee camps.

Conversely, 700,000 Jews who had been living for centuries in Arab Muslim countries fled to the new Jewish state under pressure from their host countries, which were furious over the establishment of the State of Israel and were stepping up their persecution of their Jewish minorities. (One might ask today: If multitudes of Jews could live as minorities in "Arab countries" for all those years, why should nearly two million Arab citizens living in the Israel object to its recognition as a "Jewish state"? And why should 250,000 Jewish settlers living in the West Bank be forced to leave so that the future State of Palestine can be an entirely "Arab state"? If Zionism was "racism," what is this?)

The 1967 invasion plan of the Arab nations backfired. Facing an imminent threat to its very existence, Israel struck first, repelling the invaders from its borders and moving on to capture

Gaza from Egyptian occupation and the West Bank (including Israel's ancient capital, Jerusalem) from Jordanian occupation. The lightning speed of the Six Day War (bringing to mind the six days of Creation) pointed to the hand of God—and surely God hadn't performed this marvelous feat without intending for Israelis to conquer *and settle* the land that God had given them ages and ages ago.

The victorious Israelis then proceeded to do with these conquered, "occupied territories" exactly what the Arab nations had planned to do with a conquered Israel: The Israelis treated the Arab-dominated portion of western Palestine as land without any recognized sovereignty. In fact, the United Nations never acted on any application to grant sovereignty to the West Bank (and Gaza) until September 2011, when it was asked to recognize a State of Palestine.

"We do not see it as an occupied territory because there was no recognized sovereignty there before 1948," declared Elyakim Rubenstein of the Israeli Supreme Court. "We'll stay put," said Israeli Prime Minister Levi Eshkol. "We can strangle terror in the occupied territories." His defense would be the Three No's that came out of the Arab summit in Khartoum, Sudan, in August 1967: "No peace with Israel, no negotiations with Israel, no recognition of Israel, and maintenance of the rights of Palestinian [Arab] people in their nation."[3]

By the summer of 2005, when Israel evacuated Gaza, there were 250,000 Jews living in 125 officially recognized settlements in the West Bank and 180,000 living in the area of East Jerusalem that Israel annexed in 1980.

In July 1968, a year after the loss of Gaza and the West Bank, the Palestine National Covenant was redrafted to reject the partition of Palestine which, "with the boundaries it had during the British mandate, is an indivisible territorial unit." (It is not clear whether this was meant to include eastern Palestine, now called Jordan.) The document *did* recognize the existence of Palestinian Jews, defined as those who "resided in Palestine until the

3. "Israel Says It Will Keep"

65

beginning of the Zionist invasion," without specifying when that began. Those Jews could continue to live in a future Palestinian state (as they had in Arab countries). However: *"Judaism, being a religion, is not an independent nationality. Nor do Jews constitute a single nation with an identity of its own; they are citizens of the states to which they belong."*[4]

Ironically, these words were written by Arabs who claim today that Israel has attempted to deny that Palestinian Arabs are *an independent nationality* that would *constitute a single nation with an identity of its own.*

~

Why had the Arab nations not pushed for a sovereign State of Palestine from 1948 to 1967, when they controlled Gaza and the West Bank? Wouldn't this have advanced the rights of Palestinian Arabs in *their nation*? That is a question that Palestinian Arabs are asking today, with a deep sense of resentment at having been kept as helpless pawns to be used against Israel. A common saying is that the Arabs are 'for the Palestinian cause but not for the Palestinians.' The Arab nations have encouraged the Palestinian Arabs to teach antisemitism in their schools (I witnessed this when I visited a UN school in Irbid, Jordan, in 1985), thus perpetuating their resentment in successive generations, and branding as traitors those wishing to share the land and make peace with Israel. All the while, they have cleverly used the Palestinians as terrorist proxies against Israel. The evidence that the Arab nations hated Israel more than they loved their fellow Arabs was never so clear as when they failed to come to their rescue on the battlefield. They did nothing when Israel invaded Lebanon in 1982 to drive out Palestinian Arab militias that were harassing Israelis across the border. Even when the battle was inside Palestine, when Israel invaded Gaza in 2008 to stop Hamas from firing rockets into Israel, the Arab nations did nothing. And they did nothing immediately after the IDF entered Gaza to destroy Hamas.

4. Peters, *Since Time Immemorial,* 417

While Arabs and other Muslims across the world have sympathized with the Palestinian Arabs, their leaders preferred that they remain stateless and continue to resort to terrorism against the hated Jewish state. In fact, Iran had been smuggling weapons to Hamas in Gaza—and Syria had been arming Hezbollah in Lebanon—to maintain terrorist activities against Israel. What Iran and Syria did not do was commit their own armies against Israel during its showdown against the terrorists.

At the same time, these Arabs living as refugees have given their Arab host countries reason to fear them as a people. During "Black September" 1970, the Bedouin king of Jordan expelled the PLO in a bloody crackdown, fearing a Palestinian Arab takeover. Long intent on taking over eastern Palestine, the PLO had set up political and military bases in refugee camps, from which it launched terrorist attacks against Israel. Many PLO fighters fled Jordan to Lebanon, where a new group called Black September emerged (two years later it murdered eleven Israeli athletes in Munich). A generation later Hezbollah has won political control of Lebanon and has amassed thousands of rockets aimed at Israel.

The Arabs' decades-old incremental strategy for winning all of western Palestine—by negotiating land-for-peace agreements with Israel and continuing armed struggle from there—should also raise future alarms for Jordan—as well as Lebanon and Egypt—where Palestinian Arabs might someday claim they are historically entitled to certain provinces bordering on their future State of Palestine.

Just as the wandering Jews refused to become assimilated and lose their ancient heritage, the Palestinian Arabs have maintained their identity in Arab countries and elsewhere. The difference is that unlike the Jews, whose mandate as a people goes back to Sinai and before, the "Palestinian Arabs" scarcely existed as a people with a nationalistic identity until the idea was born out of rejection by their fellow Arabs.

The Arab nations, then, have been playing with fire. Islamic dictators have long feared that Palestinian Arab fever for secular democracy could be a deadly poison to their own populations.

Even Egypt and Syria, long ruled by secular tyrants, feared an infestation of rebellious Palestinian Arabs among their population and excluded them.

But in 2011, during the "Arab Spring" revolts that began toppling Arab dictators, fear was growing in Israel that this fever would spread to the Arabs living in the West Bank and Gaza—and even to the nearly two million Arabs enjoying citizenship in Israel proper. After decades of antisemitic indoctrination in their schools, virtually all Palestinian Arabs have resented Israel's treaties with Egypt and Jordan, which were negotiated by their Arab dictators without the public's support. They also resent America's role in bringing about those treaties. In the wake of the Arab Spring, the populace in each liberated country will never forgive America for having supported their tyrant leaders for all those decades. But how would they have felt if, years earlier, the United States had invaded their sovereign Muslim soil and removed their despots, as the U.S. did in Iraq? The very thought of infidel troops on Islamic soil—for *any* purpose—is anathema to the Muslim mind, which longs for the Muslim world to be united as one.

The question, then, was: Would the Arab *people* deal more sympathetically with their Palestinian Arab brothers and sisters now that they had toppled the dictators who betrayed Palestine by making peace with Israel?

Ironically, the pan-Arab movement of the twentieth century did succeed in bringing together scores of rival Arabic tribes—but *only* under the iron fists of dictators who took over the emerging post-Ottoman states of the new Middle East. The sudden fall of any one of these dictators would produce immediate chaos, as in the case of Iraq, where the United States dethroned Saddam Hussein, only to ignite a civil war between his fellow Sunnis and the majority Shi'ites who could now take control and revenge on the Sunnis.

If anything, the long-awaited emergence of one united Arab nation from the ashes of the Turkish Ottoman Empire was held back by the very dictators of Egypt and Syria and Jordan who were hypocritically clamoring for such a unity. Government-imposed national unity proved to be an artificial blanket that concealed age-old tribal rivalries smoldering beneath, waiting to be released at this late date in history to bring chaos to the Arab streets. Libya is the most graphic example. In Syria, in fact, the ruling family actually perpetuated those divisions among its people by a strategy of "divide and conquer," keeping rival tribes at odds with each other while they lay prostrate under iron rule. And when the people rose up in rebellion, Bashar al-Assad spent a decade bombing their cities and forcing millions of his people to flee the country.

The Arab Spring was seen in 2011 as either the harbinger of a new order emerging in the Arab world—or the omen of an extended period of chaos.

Curiously, most Arabs in the Middle East—and Palestinian Arabs in particular—have proven unready for the democracy that they so fervently crave. The concept of democracy did not spring naturally from the Old Testament, the New Testament or the Quran. All three religions still look forward to a world theocracy in the end times. In fact, democracy was the slogan but never the goal of the "peace" talks toward a two-state solution. Rather, those talks now seem to have been a cloak for a one-state solution, with all of western Palestine eventually becoming the planet's twenty-third Muslim state.

The Arab "land for peace" proposals, now seen in retrospect, were calculated to fail. Consider just two of the arguments long considered inescapable:

— No Arab leader with knowledge of Middle Eastern history could possibly expect the Israelis to give up all of the occupied West Bank, the heartland of previous Jewish commonwealths under David, Solomon and the Maccabees. Without it, Israel is indefensible, with a depth as narrow as ten miles separating the West Bank from the Mediterranean. The Prime Minister's residence is barely a mile from the "green line" that once marked Israel's border of the West Bank.

— A geographically divided Palestinian State of Gaza and the West Bank would be too weak a country to thrive. Israel voluntarily drove all of the Jewish settlers out of Gaza in 2005. But since 1967 it has settled the West Bank with so many Jews—and invested so many resources in building residential and business communities and the roads and infrastructure to serve them—that a Palestinian state on the remaining Arab lands would be hopelessly decimated. As for evacuating Jewish settlers from the West Bank, it most likely cannot be done without driving the settlers to civil war. Many of them are so attached to their biblical land that they would rather live there under the Palestinian flag than return to Israel proper!

That is why in recent years so many Arab leaders, and the Palestinian Arabs themselves, had been moving away from the two-state solution and concentrating on creating one, bi-national State of Palestine (with or without the Jewish settlements remaining in place). The only role of democracy would be for the Arab population, with its higher reproduction rate, to democratically take over the country in the voting booth. It is hard to imagine Arabs governing themselves democratically in an Islamic state, or even in a secular state like the Kingdom of Jordan. This is because most Arabs in the Mideast don't have the experience of having lived in a democracy that Jews from Europe had.

Israelis have tried desperately to avoid the one-state solution. Three times they offered a Palestinian state in the West Bank and Gaza and part of the Old City of Jerusalem: At Camp David in 2000, at Taba in 2001, and in Jerusalem in 2008. The Arab negotiators walked away all three times. Why? Because—while signing cease-fires and interim agreements was easy—signing a final peace agreement ending the conflict for all time would require them to recognize a Jewish state in western Palestine.

Bi-national states have produced disappointing records, with the notable exception of Canada and possibly Belgium. Failures include Bosnia, Cyprus, Kosovo, Lebanon, Pakistan, Rwanda and Sri Lanka.

Failing to capture all of western Palestine militarily, and stalled by their own recalcitrance at the negotiating table, the Palestinian Arabs then sought statehood unilaterally through the

United Nations—without having to sign a peace agreement with Israel in return. How could the UN's declaration of a State of Palestine on paper change anything on the ground? At the very least, it would make Israel guilty of attacking a sovereign foreign country the next time it sent troops into Gaza to stop the firing of rockets into Israeli neighborhoods.

Ever since the IDF forcibly removed 8,000 Jewish settlers and gave up Gaza to Arab rule in 2005, Israel has been rewarded with rocket fire aimed at innocent civilians. Hamas took over Gaza through democratic voting and, two years later, violently expelled the Palestinian Authority from Gaza. Hamas has always been intent on creating an *Islamic* Palestine, even if it has to wage civil war against the Palestinian Authority and take from it the West Bank. Should Israel make the same mistake and unilaterally withdraw from the West Bank, where Hamas enjoys popularity among voters and could replace the Palestinian Authority's goal of a *secular* Palestine? With no trustworthy Arab partner to negotiate with, Israel continued to settle the West Bank—ancient Judea and Samaria—with Jewish families.

A peaceful resolution would have to materialize, somehow, in the distant future. . .

~

As the years have gone by, the nightmare of being labeled as "occupiers" over another people has cast a different light on Israel's lightening victory in the Six Day War, which religious Jews and evangelical Christians have always seen as evidence of the hand of God. Could a different, sinister force have been at work instead, baiting a trap from which Israel cannot extricate itself?

Surely this wasn't the first time in history that a militarily stronger people has won over a weaker people and presumed to become their benign rulers. The popular Peace Now movement in Israel struggled for years to bring justice to the Palestinian Arabs. And in a gesture toward self-autonomy for them, the Israel government brought about the creation of the Palestinian Authority, so that they could at least have their own security force and municipal home rule. This could never be enough for a people dispossessed of their land—but wasn't much of that land *purchased* from individual Arab landowners both before the 1948 war?

"The truth is that from the beginning of World War I, part of Palestine's land was owned by absentee landlords who lived in Cairo, Damascus and Beirut," writes Mitchell G. Bard, an American foreign policy analyst and executive director of the nonprofit American-Israeli Cooperative Enterprise. "About 80 percent of the Palestinian Arabs were debt-ridden peasants, semi-nomads and Bedouins. Jews actually went out of their way to avoid purchasing land in areas where Arabs might be displaced.

They sought land that was largely uncultivated, swampy, cheap and, most important, without tenants." In fact, Bard wrote, 37 percent of total immigration to pre-state Israel was by Arabs from neighboring countries "who wanted to take advantage of the higher standard of living the Jews had made possible." In the two decades leading up to the mid-1940s, he said, Arab infant mortality fell from 201 to 94 babies per thousand, and Arabs' life expectancy rose from 37 to 49 years.[5]

In 1920 David Ben-Gurion, who would become the first prime minister of Israel, said: "Under no circumstances must we touch land belonging to fellahs [peasants] or worked by them. Only if a fellah leaves his place of settlement should we offer to buy his land, at an appropriate price."[6]

Arriving in Palestine in May 1930, British diplomat John Hope Simpson observed that the Jews "paid high prices for the land, and in addition they paid to certain of the occupants of those lands a considerable amount of money which they were not legally bound to pay." The British High Commissioner to Palestine later reported: "In 1944, Jews paid between $1,000 and $1,100 per acre in Palestine, mostly for arid or semi-arid land; in the same year, rich black soil in Iowa was selling for about $110 per acre."[7]

5. "Buying Back Their Land," 1
6. "Ben-Gurion Reiterates"
7. Peters, *Since Time Immemorial,* 318

Britain's Peel Commission, rejecting Arab claims that Jews had taken their cultivated land, pointed out that "much of the land now carrying orange groves was sand dunes or swamp and uncultivated when it was purchased. There was at the time of the earlier sales little evidence that the owners possessed either the resources or training needed to develop the land."[8]

King Abdullah of Jordan remarked in his memoirs: "It is made quite clear to all, both by the map drawn by the Simpson Commission and by another compiled by the Peel Commission, that the Arabs are as prodigal in selling their land as they are in useless wailing and weeping."[9]

By 1947, about 463,000 acres of land in Palestine were in Jewish hands—387,500 acres purchased from Arabs, 30,000 acres from various churches, and 45,000 acres acquired from the British Mandatory government. Nearly three-quarters of the land was purchased from large land owners, not peasants working the land, from 1880 to 1948.

If the birth of the State of Israel in 1948 was a *nakba* (catastrophe) for Arabs living in western Palestine, it was inflicted by the neighboring Arab states, says Efraim Karsh, head of Mediterranean Studies at King's College, University of London. "Had the Arab states pressured the AHC [Arab High Command] to accept [the UN] partition resolution rather than abort it by force of arms," Karsh says, "the Palestinian tragedy would have been averted altogether."[10]

This was admitted in October 2011 by Mahmoud Abbas, president of the Palestinian Authority (and chairman of the PLO), in the wake of his request that the UN accept a State of Palestine into membership. In a rare interview with Israeli television, Abbas said this of Arab rejection of the 1947 partition plan: "It was our mistake. It was an Arab mistake as a whole." Abbas also admitted that Israeli Prime Minister Ehud Olmert had created "a very good opportunity" for peace during negotiations in May 2008 by

8. Peel Commission Report
9. Bard, *Myths and Facts*, 45
10. Karsh, "Palestine Betrayed," 34

offering to give up about 94 percent of the West Bank for a Palestinian state and to share sovereignty over Jerusalem. Just before leaving office, President George W. Bush met one-on-one with Abbas in the Oval Office and appealed with him to accept the offer.[11]

"The Palestinian stood firm, and the idea died," Condoleeza Rice, then secretary of state, wrote in her book, *No Higher Honor,* in 2011. The Prime Minister's offer was so generous that it probably would not have been approved by his parliament, the Knesset. Foreseeing this, the Palestinian Arabs could well have called the Prime Minister's bluff and, once the deal fell through, could have had a plausible reason for sparking the Second Intifada of 2008. [12]

In a *New York Times* op-ed piece earlier, on May 17, Abbas had already confessed his true motives for going to the United Nations: "Palestine's admission to the UN would pave the way for the internationalization of the conflict as a legal matter. It would pave the way for us to pursue claims against Israel at the UN, human rights treaty bodies and the International Court of Justice." [13]

Abbas, whose Palestinian Authority controls only the West Bank, included Gaza in his UN application for statehood. But Gaza is controlled by Hamas, which forced Abbas' Fatah party loyalists out of Gaza in a bloody takeover that virtually constituted a civil war among Palestinians. A cease-fire was quickly patched together for the sake of unity before the United Nations. Except for the case of the Palestinian Arabs, it is difficult to image the UN granting statehood to any people engaged in civil war and unable to govern together.

And why should Israel reward the October 7 massacre by supporting statehood?

❧

As for the morality of taking land by force and keeping it, this has always been the rule of the jungle throughout human history.

11. "Arab Rejection"
12. Rice, *No Higher Honor*
13. Abbas, "The Long Overdue Palestinian State"

Nobody gives away land (except Israel, which voluntarily returned the Sinai to Egypt after dismantling Jewish settlements there).

Nor is this the first time in history that Samaria has been the scene of conquest and resettlement of populations. From 724 to 721 BC, Assyria deported 27,290 residents, most of them Jewish, from Samaria and replaced them with captives from other regions. (Among the newcomers were the Sepharvim—who burned their children in the fire as sacrifices to their pagan gods. Such an abomination would doom them—as it had doomed the Canaanites before them—to be dispossessed of their land by God.) Samaritans at the time of Christ were descendants of Assyrian colonists who intermarried with Jews who had returned to Samaria.

The twelfth century biblical scholar Rashi made a statement about the ancient Canaanite inhabitants of Samaria and Judea that could also apply today to the Arab Palestinians:

"If the nations accuse Israel of banditry, of illegitimately seizing the lands of the seven nations of Canaan, Israel will say: 'The entire universe belongs to God. He created it and granted its territory to whomever He deemed fit. It was His desire to give it to them [the Canaanites], and it was later His desire to take it from them and grant it to us.'"[14]

And then God allowed it to be taken away from the Jews . . . who wandered the earth for 2,000 years and finally won it back in 1948 and in 1967.

While the Arabs had no intention of sharing the land they hoped to take from Israel in the Six Day War, Israel not only withdrew from Gaza but allowed the Palestinian Arabs to remain and share the West Bank with Jewish settlers. At last count, there were 2.5 million people living in the West Bank—83 percent of them Palestinian Arabs and just 17 percent of them Jewish settlers, according to United Nations sources.

Why won't the Palestinian Arabs recognize Israel as a *Jewish* state? Because Israel proper already has nearly two million Arab citizens whose families never fled the land. (Isn't it odd, though, that Israel's Arab citizens are seldom referred to as *Palestinians*?

14. Kahanov, "Confronting Chutzpah with Chutzpah"

When did being refugees become a decisive factor in defining a nation's bloodline?)

Creation of a State of *Palestine*—the first ever in history—has traditionally been viewed as inevitable. But for the record, the region that was renamed *Palestine* nearly 2,000 years ago by the Romans has been carved up in modern times as follows: Jordan, 37,737 square miles; Israel, 7,992; West Bank, 2,165; Gaza, 140.

What is the territorial breakdown between Arabs and Jews on the West Bank (and in East Jerusalem?).In recent years, there were reportedly 271,400 Jews living in 121 settlements spread throughout the West Bank, plus 191,000 living in settlements around Jerusalem, for a total of 462,400 Jews.

The separation barrier (which *in only some places* is a solid wall) that Israel constructed to keep suicide bombs out of Israel was placed mostly east of the so-called "green line," which was the 1949 armistice boundary between Israel and the West Bank. If that barrier were accepted as a final boundary, it would bring 80 of the settlements—containing 385,000 Jews—into Israel proper. That would leave just 77,400 Jews to evacuate from just 41 settlements to make a State of Palestine *Judenrein*.

The Jewish settlements actually are built on less than 3 percent of the West Bank. But the extensive network of "by-pass" roads linking the settlements (each with buffer zones of 50 to 75 yards) take up 40 percent of the land.. For security reasons, Arabs aren't allowed on 500 miles of "by-pass" roads. Israel has built about 50 miles of "fabric of life" roads connecting Arab settlements, including about 60 tunnels and underpasses.

How the descendants of Abraham are to live in peace on this land is proving to be the impossible riddle of our time. Only the God of Abraham can solve it peacefully—and only the Messiah can bring these brothers and sisters back together, at last.

7

No Place to Call Their Own

THREE-QUARTERS OF A CENTURY after the Israeli War of Independence, the Arabs who fled from Palestine still have not been assimilated by the 22 Arab counties in the Middle East. Instead, the Palestinian Arabs have become the modern counterpart in the Arab world to what the Jews had been throughout history—a scattered people without a homeland, refusing to be absorbed into other cultures.

It is now clear that Palestinian Arabs are different from other Arabs, and that they blame the Arab governments for their continuing statelessness. Nor did they expect Arab nations to come to the rescue of Arabs living in Gaza after the October 7 attack on Israel. And if Arab nations should pitch in to rebuild Gaza, it will be only because they want Palestinian Arabs to be confined there, unable to emigrate and cause civil unrest in Arab countries.

How did this happen?

When the Zionist movement was beginning to stir in the 1800s to reclaim the Jewish ancestral homeland in Palestine, a spirit of nationalism was also wakening among the nomadic Arabs who had been living in Palestine, and particularly those living in lands surrounding Palestine.

The Egyptians, Syrians and Lebanese did not gain statehood immediately after the collapse of the Turkish Ottoman Empire at the end of the First World War. It was a long struggle, but they succeeded .

Only the Palestinian Arabs have failed to gain statehood.

The resurrected State of Israel arose from its 2,000-year-old ashes in western Palestine in 1948.

The two-state proposal for western Palestine began with the British, who administered all of Palestine under a mandate of the League of Nations from 1917. In their Balfour Declaration that year, they put themselves in the untenable position of promising the Jews a national homeland and the Palestinian Arabs an independent state in the western one-third of Palestine.

The eastern two-thirds of Palestine they gave in 1947 to the Bedouin leader who had helped them during World War II. Thus was born Transjordan, now Jordan, on the east bank of the Jordan River. Displaced Palestinian Arabs make up 70 percent of the population. But nobody refers to Jordan as "Palestine."

And what of western Palestine? That same year the UN drew a map proposing a Jewish state and an Arab state. The Palestinian Jews accepted; the unorganized Palestinian Arabs had no voice in the matter, as the Arab nations immediately rejected any Jewish state in the region.

When the British withdrew in May 1948 and several Arab armies rushed into the land, the Jews managed to gain control of their share of the UN partition map, plus Galilee and the eastern branch of Gaza.

Egypt took over Gaza and Jordan took over Samaria and Judea, on the west bank of the Jordan River. For the next 19 years neither nation moved to establish an independent Palestinian Arab state.

The Balfour Declaration had promised the Jews "the establishment in Palestine of a national home for the Jewish people." But it stipulated that nothing would be done "which may prejudice the civil and religious rights of existing non-Jewish communities."

When the Second World War broke out, and the Nazi Holocaust, the British played the Jews and Arabs against each other, to keep Jewish fighters and resources on the Allies' side, and to keep the Arab people from joining the Nazi side. While millions of Jews were perishing in Europe, the British were promising relief but keeping the lid on Jewish immigration to Palestine, because the Arabs were growing restless over the swelling Jewish population.

Germany was promising statehood to the Arabs if they would join the Axis. A Nazi foothold in the Middle East could have meant control of the Suez Canal and victory against the Allies. And as we have seen, the Grand Mufti of Jerusalem was allied with the Nazis.

After Israel was resurrected in 1948, some 700,000 Jews were forced to flee to Israel from the Arab countries in the Mideast and North Africa where they had lived as minorities for centuries. They had stubbornly refused to be assimilated with the Arabs who ruled them.

Similarly, those Palestinian Arab refuges who made it to Egypt, Jordan, Lebanon and Syria have failed to assimilate. Clearly, those Arab states have not made a serious effort to integrate them into their society

Palestinian Arabs—coming out of a vaguely defined region as opposed to a real country—scarcely existed as a people with a nationalist identity until the idea was born out of rejection by both Israelis and Arabs. There had never been a country called Palestine, nor a people called Palestinians, until the PLO declared a new nationality in 1964 and sought to make western Palestine the site of the world's first State of Palestine.

And so, as a nation without a country of its own, Palestinian Arabs have a great deal in common with the Palestinian Jews with whom they have been at war since 1948. Many of them have boasted to me that they are indeed "the Jews of the Arab world."

While they can hardly pretend to love the Jews, Palestinian Arabs have lived in close proximity to Jews for so long that they know the Jews better than do their Arab brothers who live in their own countries.

The flight of these Arabs during Israel's War of Independence has usually been blamed on the Zionists and the bungling British who abruptly departed in 1948. But Palestinian Arabs also blame the leaders of those Arab countries for their predicament. Egypt,

Jordan, Syria, Lebanon, Iraq, Saudi Arabia and Yemen formed the Arab League after World War II and were the Arab powers that Britain chose to deal with instead of the stateless Arabs.

Arab refugees whom I have interviewed declare that hatred for the Jews and Israel was always more important to the Arab governments than helping the Palestinian Arabs. Prolonging the refugee problem has served to keep Israel on the defensive.

While their Arab brothers and sisters throughout the Mideast sympathize with them, Palestinian Arabs say that Arab leaders do not want them to have their own state—and fear their very presence within their borders. In fact, the Palestine Liberation Organization attempted to topple Jordanian King Hussein and seize control of the country, but thousands of them were massacred, during "Black September" 1970.

Today, Palestinian Arabs are known as the most well-educated people of the Arab world. Even while living in refugee camps, they have educated their children and sent them to the far corners of the Arab world to seek their fortune—to Amman, Jordan; to Saudi Arabia; to the oil-rich Arab principalities of the Persian Gulf—and also to the United States.

Like the Jews before them, the Palestinian Arabs have found that adversity can be the mother of inner growth. Without a land of their own, and with their Arab hosts suspicious of their motives and jealous of their every minor success, they have turned inward and nurtured a nationalism in their hearts and in their minds.

According to the Old Testament, which is the bedrock of Judaism and Christianity and a critical source of the Quran, the Jews and Arabs are blood brothers. And Muslim Arabs claim that it was Ishmael, not Isaac, whom Abraham was willing to sacrifice on Mount Moriah.

8

What Some Palestinian Arabs Did to Palestinian Jews

SOME PALESTINIAN ARAB APOLOGISTS have claimed that they are descendants of the ancient Canaanites, who lived in Palestine before the Jewish arrival. This is patently false. Yet Hamas—by embedding its fighters in the civilian population, thus using them as human shields—in effect has sacrificed its own people as did the Canaanites, who cast their babies into the fire to appease their pagan gods. And now Hamas terrorists have burned Jewish babies in ovens, in front of their parents, as a demonic sacrifice of sorts.

Two months after the October 7 massacre, 90 percent of Palestinian Arabs believed that "Hamas did not commit the atrocities seen in the videos" of attacks on civilians that day, according to the Palestinian Center for Policy and Survey Research. Some 85 percent of those polled said they had not even seen the video footage. Khalil Shikaki, director of the organization, attributed it to a lack of coverage in the Arab media.

However, Michael Milshtein, head of the Forum for Palestinians Studies at the Dayan Center at Tel Aviv University, questioned this. "Hamas filmed everything, and the videos were widely circulated," he said.[1]

1. "For Most Palestinians"

In early December 2023, United Nations officials were given accounts about sexual mutilation of women by Hamas. Army reservist Shari Mendes, whose IDF rabbinical unit worked with the bodies at the IDF's Sura base, said: "Our team commander saw several female soldiers who were shot in the crotch—intimate parts/vagina—or shot in the breast."

She went on, "Our unit has seen bodies that were beheaded or had limbs cut off, mutilated. Charred remains arrived that had to be identified and prepared for burial. These bodies were burned beyond recognition, often without arms or legs; they did not resemble anything human." The rest of her presentation was even more graphic. [2]

Members of Congress and other dignitaries reportedly were shocked and moved to tears when shown images compiled by the Israeli government

"Dead silence interrupted by anguished howls," wrote Gil Zohar in *Jerusalem Report*. "That was the reaction on October 23 among the 200 foreign journalists present at an IDF briefing (who were) shown a harrowing 43-minute compilation of Hamas bodycam videos. . . Overwhelmed with grief, some journalists stepped out of the auditorium early." [3]

One of them, Ron Cantor, who heads the Christian TV station Shelanu in Israel, told me in November 2023 that he had just viewed those images.

"I was invited with other faith-based journalists in Israel to view the footage that Israel had recovered from the bodies of Hamas terrorists," he wrote. "What I will share is unpleasant, but it must be told," he went on. "Already, people have forgotten the Hamas atrocities of October 7th and the 242 primarily Israeli hostages. A young girl at a pro-Palestinian rally was asked what she thought of the Hamas invasion of Israel—*she didn't even know about it*. This was just a few weeks after the attack."

He continued:

---

2. Lazaroff, "Female Soldiers Shot in Crotch," 5
3. Zohar, "Media Shocked"

"In the footage, I saw a father and his two sons run outside to their safe room in their underwear at 6:30 a.m. when sirens alerted them of incoming rockets. Moments later, Hamas terrorists came in and threw a grenade into the safe room. The father stumbled out half dead, and they shot him. They pulled the kids over their dead father and took them to the kitchen. These children were in complete shock, crying over their father's death. 'They killed Abba!' one cried. The other children had been blinded in one eye. But the terrorist was hungry. He rummaged through the refrigerator and seemed to ask the kids if there was something to eat. He took out a Coke and began to drink.

"The mother came home later with security forces and found her dead husband. She collapsed. I don't know what happened with the boys. I watched as a dog came to protect his family, and the terrorists shot him. The dog kept coming. They shot him until he was dead. I watched as they searched and found those hiding and shot them in cold blood. Motorists who had no idea of the Hamas invasion were shot dead as they approached the terrorists. Bodies fell out of cars, dead.

"U.S. Secretary of State Antony Blinken told of a woman having her breasts cut off and her husband's eye gauged out before they were both killed. A soldier gave eyewitness testimony of finding a baby in a burning oven. They obviously cooked the child in front of the parents before killing them both.

"The terrorists themselves were overjoyed. I have never seen such happy people. If you didn't know they were committing acts of barbarism, you would think they were at a wedding or sporting event. One called home to Gaza to his parents. He told them he was calling from the phone of a woman he killed. 'Your son is a hero. . . I killed ten Jews with my bare hands,' he boasted.

"These savages have found friends on college campuses in the U.S. and on the streets of Europe. At George Washington University they projected on a building the words that call for another Jewish genocide, 'Glory to our martyrs. Free Palestine from the river to the sea.' At Columbia University, Professor Joseph Massad called the slaughter 'awesome.' Another professor at Cornell,

Russell Rickford, said he was 'exhilarated' by the October 7th attack by Hamas and called Israelis 'irredeemable excrement.'

"In Sydney, Australia, crowds gathered at the Sydney Opera House and chanted, 'Gas the Jews.' A Harvard Task Force was formed to protect *pro-Hamas* students, and a letter was written by professors rebuking their president for condemning antisemitism. People rejoiced at the news (of the slaughter) on the streets of Berlin, Toronto, Paris, and right here in London."

Cantor then addressed the Christian world:

"But where will the Church stand? When the Messiah returns to Jerusalem, the Bible says he will separate the people of the nations as sheep and goats. He will ask them how they treated his brothers—the Jewish people. Yes, the Sheep and the Goats prophecy is about the nations' treatment of Israel. Zechariah 14:16 says that all the survivors of nations will be summoned to Jerusalem to worship the Messiah. It is then that he will ask, 'How did you treat the least of my brothers?'"

Then he issued this challenge:

"God is using Israel as a test for the world. Where will you stand? Israel has very few friends worldwide, but she has the Church. We will not give up until Hamas is destroyed and every hostage is returned! We speak to Hamas and say in the spirit, 'Let God's people go!'"[4]

---

4. Ron Cantor, email to author, November 2023

9

Jewish and Arab Brothers
in Messiah

ONE MORNING AN ISRAELI Jew named Yossi got out of his cab and walked into the Olive Tree, a hotel on the invisible border between an Orthodox Jewish neighborhood and Arab East Jerusalem. He was looking for an American couple. He didn't know their name, but he was certain that Yeshua (Jesus) of Nazareth would send them to him.

My wife and I came out of the elevator and began walking toward the lobby. Yossi was walking toward us from the opposite direction—down a long corridor. Our eyes met as we all reached the lobby, and now the three of us were standing still, facing each other.

"Here I am," Yossi told us. "Where do you want to go first?"

Startled, we told him we hadn't called anybody—but we *did* need a cab.

Yossi just smiled and led us outside to his cab. After taking us to a bank in Rechavia, Yossi suggested a souvenir shop nearby, on Metudela Street, that was owned by a friend. When we got there the owner, Jonathan, said he too was a believer in Yeshua, the Messiah. Jonathan had recently been forced to move his shop from a busier part of Jerusalem because the Orthodox Jews found out about his faith and organized a boycott. (Three years later, on our return, he had again moved his shop.)

Jonathan then proceeded to show us his rugs, produced by Jewish families that had brought their age-old craft from Iran and needed the money. All of them are Christian believers, he said, and they secretly attend Jewish messianic services in someone's house in Modi'in. This ancient town was the birthplace of the Maccabees, who in the second century before Christ conducted guerrilla warfare against the Syrian soldiers who had set up a pagan altar in Modi'in and pressured Jews to abandon Judaism in favor of Greek pagan customs. The Syrians had even profaned the Temple, erecting a statue of Zeus on the altar. The Maccabee victory is celebrated on Hanukkah.

The *Messianic Times* lists 230 Messianic synagogues in 30 countries, including 27 in Israel. An estimated 15,000 Jews in Israel believe in Messiah Yeshua, some privately to avoid persecution, some boldly in public. Ultra-Orthodox Jews have sometimes been violent in their opposition, such as fire bombing a building in Kirykat Arba, and sending a package with a bomb, which severely injured a boy when he opened it at his kitchen table.

Seating me and Shirah now on two chairs decked like thrones, Jonathan served us hot tea with mint leaves freshly picked that morning from his mother's garden. After purchasing a large rug, some souvenirs, and a large bottle of holy oil for use by our congregation back home, we returned to the cab, and Yossi drove us to the Mount of Olives. There we had a spectacular view of the Old City as seen by Yeshua from here, in his favorite place of prayer. At an Arab bazaar, Yossi introduced us to Shlomo, another Jewish believer. Shlomo sold my wife a beautiful green-and-cream gown that had been sewn by female soldiers to support the families of IDF casualties.

Yossi then drove us to the Garden of Gethsemane, where the Lord spent his last night before his arrest. Some of the olive trees were several feet in diameter, and might been here as saplings on that night, two thousand years ago.

All over Israel, motorists are in such an impatient hurry that they are constantly honking their horns at each other. Shirah remarked that they were probably leaning on their horns to relieve the tension on these dangerous streets and highways, and that it was comical, in a way, as if they were all honking their nation's real national anthem. Surely, Shabbat—or Shabbos, as the Ashkenazi from Europe pronounce it—is the key to Israeli time: Without a mandatory shutdown once a week, hurly-burly Israeli society would surely have burned itself out by now.

Back at Jonathan's souvenir shop, we all went inside and took a break. Another Jewish cab driver, named Adam, showed up. After being introduced to this Jewish believer in Yeshua, I excused myself and went to find my wife at the other end of the shop.

"You've got to meet this man," I told her. "He looks to me like the young David—I think he's a born leader."

Adam warmly embraced us, then prayed with us—blessing us with "joy, happiness, love and peace." Later Shirah told me that she had felt the anointing coming down on us as this charismatic man prayed.

Several days later, we were standing outside the hotel, looking for a cab, when Adam drove up in his Mercedes and greeted us as an old friend. He offered to drive us to Bethlehem.

"Today," he said grandly as we drove off, "will be your first real day in Israel!"

Outside the walled Old City, our cab stopped for a light at a congested corner—and here a moment of truth forced itself on my wife: Our cabbie was waiting to turn left, and a cab in the oncoming lane—driven by a man wearing an Arab headdress—was at a standstill, facing us. The two cab drivers looked into each other's faces for a long time. Shirah told me later that she found it heartbreaking. She could see in both their faces a kind of tenderness, a helplessness over the circumstances that paralyzed them, like their ancestral brothers Isaac and Ishmael.

On our way to Bethlehem, the IDF halted us at one of several West Bank security checkpoints and asked to see our passports. Once we entered Bethlehem, Adam stopped his cab outside an

Arab shop, the King Solomon Bazaar, and—without explanation—
went inside. He soon returned with a Palestinian Arab named
George. He would be our guide at the Church of the Nativity.

We passed a field—now built up with modern housing—
where it is said that Ruth met Boaz, her future husband. George
quoted from the Book of Ruth, where the Moabite woman said to
Naomi, her Jewish mother-in-law, "Your people will be my people,
your God will be my God. Where you die I will die, and there
I will be buried." Then George added an Arab touch, "Your land
will be my land." At Shepherds Field we got out of the cab and
walked down to a cave similar to where Yeshua was born; this one
had a manger carved out of stone. One the way, I tasted brown
carob seeds hanging from a tree and thought of the *carubi* that my
grandmother had eaten as candy in Sicily.

After our tour of the Church of the Nativity, we all slowly am-
bled back to the cab, singing a hymn that we all happened to know,
and Adam drove us back to the King Solomon Bazaar. Inside Adnan, the owner, served us refreshments and ordered a falafel lunch.
Adam and Shirah and I dipped our pita bread into the hummus—
made of mashed chickpeas, oil, lemon juice and crushed sesame
seeds—and scooped up chunks of tomatoes, pepper and onions.
Then we looked over jewelry and Christian souvenirs.

George, a lifelong Greek Orthodox Christian, supplies the
shop with religious ikons from his relatives, who need money.
Adnan, born and raised a Roman Catholic, said he was born again
five years ago and stopped drinking.

Adam the cabbie said he had been drug-free for the past six
years and ten months.

According to George, 50 percent of Israel's Palestinian Arab
Christians are Eastern Orthodox, 35 percent are Catholic, and
many of the others are Lutheran Evangelical believers.

Among Jewish believers, Adam attends Congregation
HaCarmel in Haifa, one of the larger messianic synagogues. Traditional Jews in Israel and America balk at accepting messianic con-
gregations as "synagogues," looking on them instead as churches
with Jewish trappings. Messianic Jews long to be accepted as a

legitimate denomination of Judaism. In fact, they see themselves as the latter-day reincarnation of the Early Church in Jerusalem, which was composed entirely of Jews who continued to worship in the Temple in spite of the ongoing persecution of the followers of Yeshua. Never disqualified as legitimate Jews, their congregation at Jerusalem nevertheless fled across the Jordan before the Roman soldiers came to destroy the Temple.

We spent quite a bit of money at Adnan's shop. As we drove out of Bethlehem, Adam remarked that our purchases today had come just in time for Adnan to pay the rent and utilities on his shop.

Back in Jerusalem, after Adam had dropped us off, I said to Shirah: "Isn't it amazing? We just had a Jewish cabbie drive us American tourists to an Arab souvenir shop so he could share his good fortune with the shop owner and his tour guide friend. I mean, who would have thought of such a thing as Jews and Arabs working in cahoots to support each other in the tourist trade? These three citizens of Israel have found the answer—and those poor 'peace negotiators' haven't got a clue!"

"What finally brought them together was their belief in the Messiah of Israel," my wife said. "That's the only way there will ever be peace in the Holy Land."[1]

> For he himself is our peace, who has made the two one and has destroyed the barrier, the dividing wall of hostility . . . His purpose was to create in himself one new man out of the two, thus making peace, and in this one body to reconcile both of them to God through the cross, by which he put to death their hostility.
> – Eph 2:14–16 (NIV)

This is one of the joys of being Christian Zionists. And we are not alone.

---

1. Cardinale, *The Red Heifer*, 289–292

10

Christian Zionism Since
the 1967 Mideast War

THE DRAMATIC RISE OF support for Israel by Christians came after the recovery of Jerusalem in 1967, which was seen as another
miracle, echoing the extraordinary victory of Israel's war for independence in 1948.

Religious Jews, evangelical Christians, Catholic charismatics—and Jewish and Gentile members of the Messianic Jewish
synagogues that have sprung up around the world during the ensuing years—all believe that Israel's recovery of Jerusalem in 1967
was a miracle. If we were to take each group at its word, we would
conclude that God either started or quickened several religious
movements simultaneously during that decade:

— The *baal t'shuvah* revival, which saw Orthodox rabbis searching out fallen-away Jews (a historic first for rabbinic Judaism)
  after the Six Day War. Many saw the recovery of Jerusalem as
  the dawning of the messianic age.

— The Catholic charismatic renewal, a lay movement of prayer
  meetings featuring Scripture, music, petitions, testimonies,
  laying of hands for healings, tongues, words of prophecy, and
  high praises of God. Many became Christian Zionists.

— The "born again" movement, giving a heretofore obscure scriptural name to the rising phenomenon of nominal Protestants suddenly giving their lives to Christ and going on to spread the Word. Many became Christian Zionists. I personally trace it back to 1976, when Chuck Colson published his book, *Born Again,* after serving a prison term for his part in the Watergate scandal.

— The Messianic Jewish Alliance of America, a successor to the Hebrew Christian Alliance (most of whose members perished in the Holocaust), came into its own soon after 1967 and went on to form Messianic Jewish synagogues around the world. Springing from evangelical origins, the movement features Jewish vestments and Jewish-flavored services (adding to the Torah and Haftorah readings the *B'rith Hadoshah* reading of the week each Sabbath). It sees itself as a latter-day replication of the Early Church, which was actually a Jewish cult. MJAA has raised millions of dollars in material and monetary aid for Israel, and Orthodox Israelis have come to accept this aid less and less grudgingly, no longer suspecting that MJAA has a missionizing agenda.

— The evangelical world at large has been transformed into a major Christian Zionist force since the Six Day War. Evangelicals continue flocking to Israel even when periodic rises in violence occur, while other Christians (and Jews) stay home. Their devotion to Israel has begun to wane only in recent years, with the rise of Christian concerns over the Palestinian Arabs living in the Judea and Samaria (the "Israeli occupied West Bank"). In fact, the Jewish settlements have become a major stumbling block to peace, if only because the Zionist dream cannot be fulfilled until Israelis act justly toward the "strangers in their midst," as God commanded three dozen times in the first five books of Moses. Christian Zionism has long supported the Jewish settlement movement in the West Bank.

The ever-lurching peace process must also be considered, with an eye toward analyzing its long-term meaning, guided by the benefit of hindsight. I have interviewed Arab citizens of Israel during my five visits to Israel, as well as Palestinian refugees in Jordan, and can tell their story of expulsion and occupation.

The varied and fluctuating attitudes of Israelis toward the settlements in Samaria and Judea (on the west bank of the Jordan River) are fascinating, as well as heart-rending. The Peace Now movement of mostly secular Israelis has been dealt a crushing, demoralizing blow by the failure of the peace process. In particular, Israel's unilateral evacuation of settlers from Gaza in 2005 backfired, with a Hamas-ruled neighbor intent on harassing Israeli civilians with rockets in hopes of driving them out of Palestine. Peaceniks can no longer push for even partial withdrawal from the West Bank, lest Hamas take over there as well and make life impossible for Israelis living in major population centers a few short miles away from a future Palestinian state.

At the other end of the Israeli political spectrum are the spiritual descendants of Rabbi Meir Kahane, whom I interviewed extensively before he was assassinated by an Arab in 1990. Kahane launched the Kach party and was elected to the Knesset with an agenda to transfer Arabs from the West Bank to Jordan, by force and/or monetary compensation– and even to revoke the citizenship of Arab Israelis who have always lived in Israel unless they swore an oath of allegiance to the Jewish state. Rabbi Kahane had a great following in Israel and the United States; in fact I covered him several times when he spoke in Buffalo.

Kahanism lives on in the settler movement, whose most radical elements are behind the "price tag" vandalism of Arab property, not only in the West Bank but also in Israel. They have been vandalizing Israeli military vehicles and facilities, in retaliation for IDF enforcement of court orders favoring Arabs. Many Israelis fear that these settler vandals, in effect, are rehearsing for a civil war within Zionism..

Yet I have met many Israeli Arabs who want nothing more than peace with Israel. One friend I try to visit whenever I'm in

Jerusalem is Ismael Obydat, an engineer/architect/inventor whose tiny office is upstairs from Munir's falafel stand, just inside Jaffa Gate in the Old City. Ismael, who was injured playing football in his youth, has invented a game called Fireball—a non-contact sport in which two teams vie for control of the ball while standing in 15-by-15 meter squares, forming a checkerboard on a huge field of grass. The object of the game is to avoid having the ball land in your square, whereupon a referee cries "Fireball!" A perfect metaphor for Arab-Israeli violence. So respected is Ismael Obydat that he is invited to take part in Israel's annual independence day ceremonies as a representative of the Palestinian Arabs.

At the center of all this is the Temple Mount (known to Muslims as the Haram al-Sharif, the Noble Sanctuary), the jewel of the Old City of Jerusalem that was captured in June 1967. My first book, *The Red Heifer: A Jewish Cry for Messiah*, which I began researching in at Mishkenot Sha'ananim in Jerusalem in 1998, explored the current search by ultra-Orthodox radicals for a young, unblemished female cow whose ashes are required in Numbers 19 for purification of the priests before entering the Temple—which they intend to rebuild on or near the spot where the Muslim Dome of the Rock has stood for the past 1300 years. The Talmud says there were nine red heifers from the time of Moses to the destruction of the Temple by the Romans in 70 AD—and that the tenth red heifer someday will herald the coming of Messiah.

In addition to the fascinating facts about the red heifer and the controversy over the dangerous movement to reclaim the Temple Mount from its Muslim overseers, we must dwell on many spiritual reflections of the red heifer in Christianity. For example, the red heifer was the only animal that had to be sacrificed outside the city gates (on the Mount of Olives, in fact, where Jesus often prayed)—foreshadowing the sacrifice of the Lamb of God outside the gates, on Golgotha. Also, Numbers 19 warns that the rabbi who distributes the ashes to purify those about to enter (or rebuild) the Temple will himself be made impure, bringing to mind how the innocent Lamb of God, perfect without blemish, "was made sin for us" in the process of releasing us from sin. (2 Cor 5:21)

Rabbis refer to "the mystery of the red heifer," for this is a law that is impossible for man to fully understand—but which radical ultra-Orthodox are willing to follow, no matter the consequences. In fact, proponents of tearing down the Dome of the Rock often speak of how a regional religious war would "bring the Messiah"— a concept strangely similar to the view of Islamic radicals (particularly in Iran) who teach that a world conflict will bring the Mahdi, or Muslim messiah, to conquer the world for Islam. And so, we are dealing with religious fundamentalism in all its forms. The coming of a messianic figure, moreover, is the key unifying feature of all those groups.

Meanwhile, the *baal t'shuvah* Jews who have returned to their faith since 1967 are growing more and more eager for the Messiah to come. Living in North Buffalo for many years, I had the opportunity to observe the attitude of Orthodox Jews whose neighborhood synagogues I often visited and whose friendship I cultivated.

The Chasidic Jews spring from a movement going back to the late 1700s in eastern Europe. Chasidim emphasize devoutness in worship, even dancing before the Lord as King David did. In addition to the Torah study that is emphasized by other Orthodox, the Chasidim stress closeness to God—a sort of Jewish version of the charismatic movement in Christianity. Some of them seem more devout toward the Messiah they have never known than are many Christians who know him as Jesus. Many in the Lubavitch sect of Chasidism, by the way, are convinced that their beloved (and final) Rebbe, Menachem Schneerson, will rise from the dead as their messiah, if only Jews will come back to God in our time. Their idea of a dying messiah who rises from the dead—which is anathema to other Jews but not grounds for excommunication—gives living proof that the concept was not an invention of the Gentile church.

Charismatics, born-agains, Messianic Jews and evangelical Christians under discussion here all believe that these historic developments reveal the hand of the God of Israel as he re-enters Jewish history, in the wake of the Holocaust, and prepares to judge the nations that oppose his people and his gospel and sends back Yeshua of Nazareth.

11

God's Plan to Sift the Tares from the Wheat

ISRAEL WILL BE THE most polarizing issue in the world in the final days.

A spiritual sifting is going on in Israel today, as the God of Israel prepares the Chosen People for Messiah's coming. God is pressuring Israeli Jews to take a stand on the Torah, to separate those who truly love the Lord from those who persist in their secular delusions.

Israel was founded in 1948 by secular Jews hoping to create their own millennium in the Promised Land without waiting for the Messiah to come. Orthodox Jews have called this a serious mistake and are longing for Messiah to come and make the Zionist dream a spiritual reality.

True, thousands of Israelis have accepted Yeshua of Nazareth as their Messiah, many of them openly in spite of persecution by the Orthodox. But hundreds of thousands of religious Jews are waiting with growing fervor for the unnamed Messiah to come. And a growing number of them are becoming secret believers in Yeshua.

It is ironic that 2,000 years after the atonement and resurrection of Yeshua, the largest group of Jews in Israel who truly long for Messiah's coming are the Orthodox—the descendants of the Pharisees who had so viciously opposed Yeshua.

The Jewish people have survived 3,500 years because they were united, but today Israel is suffering a painful process of disunity. Yet for those who know the Scriptures—whether they be Christian believers or Orthodox Jews—it is clear that the arrival of Messiah must be preceded by a sifting of God's people to determine who truly loves him and who does not.

The rabbis teach that Messiah will come when the world is either entirely righteous or entirely wicked. If all are wicked, there will no longer be any reason for Messiah to delay coming and judging the world. If all are righteous, Messiah must immediately come and rule during a millennium of world peace.

I have asked several Orthodox rabbis whether there might be a third possibility in this "zero sum" game: What if the world were polarized between those fully religious and those stubbornly pagan who openly hate God, with nobody left sitting on the fence? Yes, the rabbis replied—this would bring Messiah.

One of them was Rabbi Heschel Greenberg, the longtime dean of the Chasidim in Buffalo. I asked him about this during his talk at Temple Beth Zion on August 12, 2018. "It says in the Talmud that there are two ways for Moshiach to come—either we're all bad or we're all good," he replied. "But if things get so bad because of the polarization, and we're all ready to kill each other and destroy each other, then Moshiach will have to come and save us from ourselves."[1]

Yeshua asked the disciples, "Do you suppose that I came to bring peace on earth? I tell you, not at all, but rather division . . . father will be divided against son . . . mother against daughter . . ." (Luke 12:51–53) He was predicting what would happen when some Jews accepted him and others did not. And it came true during his days on earth. But the division would widen over the ensuing centuries.

During my travels to Israel over the past 40 years, I have witnessed the gulf widening between religious and secular Jews,

1. Greenberg, "Jewish Unity" lecture

particularly in Jerusalem, the Holy City where it all began (and where Scripture says it will all end).

～

A controversial passage of Scripture occurs at Galatians 6:16, where the Apostle Paul writes: "And as many as walk according to this rule, peace and mercy be upon them, and upon the Israel of God." (NKJV) The Amplified Bible goes even further: "Peace and mercy be upon all who walk by this rule [who discipline themselves and conduct their lives by this principle], and upon the [true] Israel of God (Jewish believers)."

In his letter to the Romans, the Apostle Paul wrote: "Not all who are descended from Israel (Jacob) are [the true] Israel. . . . That is, it is not the children of the body [Abraham's natural descendants] who are God's children, but it is the children of the promise who are counted as [Abraham's true descendants]. (Rom 9:6 and 8, AMP) The promise of blessings that God made to Abraham was to apply to both the descendants of his and Sarah's Jewish son Isaac and his son Ishmael, whose mother was the Gentile bond woman Hagar.

Based on imperfect interpretations of these Scriptures, the church for centuries has been plagued by "replacement theology," the notion that God is finished with his once Chosen People because only Gentile Christians have been a light to the nations by preaching the gospel. But both the Old and New Testaments make it clear that the Jews will always be the Chosen People. "For the gifts and the calling of God are irrevocable [for He does not withdraw what He has given, nor does He change His mind about those to whom He sends His call]." (Rom 11:29, AMP) In the final days, 144,000 missionaries "from every tribe of the sons of Israel" will herald the coming of the Messiah, Jesus Christ (Rev 7:4). They will be religious Jews—descendants of the Pharisees—and already untold thousands of them are secret believers in Israel and America.[2]

---

2. Cardinale, *The Pharisees Are Coming to Jesus*

~

On another occasion Rabbi Greenberg spoke on the role of the Messiah according to his Lubavitcher Chasidic sect, whose teaching wing is Chabad. The Messiah is alive on the Earth, waiting to redeem the Jewish people and bring peace to the world, he said. He hastily added that every generation has had a prospective Messiah waiting to be called, should the world be ready for it.

"The Talmud," he said, "makes it very clear that there was a Moshiach from the time the Temple was destroyed [70 AD]. And in every generation, the Talmud intimates, there is a Moshiach."

Rabbi Greenberg went on: "Every day that goes by and Moshiach has not arrived, his coming is that much more likely. But it's not just based on time. It's also based on accomplishment."

Human accomplishment in the form of *mitzvahs*—good deeds and otherwise following God's commandments—can hasten the coming of the Messiah, he said. "Every time you do a mitzvah, you change the world permanently. You leave an indelible mark on the world that can never be changed. . . . When enough good will have been done, then Moshiach will have to come."

On that day, I would add, the battle will be resolved between those who truly love God and those who truly hate God.[3]

~

Today fallen-away Jews are returning to their religion. And they often do so in defiance of a secularized community that lost its faith in the God of Israel following the Emancipation during the early 1800s and Holocaust from 1933 to 1945. The Lord is working today to reverse the gravest religious apostasy in Jewish history.

The revival of Judaism after the Six Day War, when Jerusalem was restored to Jewish control after nearly 2,000 years, caused separations in many Jewish families. Rabbis were walking the streets of Jerusalem, searching for secular Jews to invite home for

---

3. Cardinale, "Rabbi at UB Explains Role of Messiah"

Shabbat. This Jewish revival pitted young returning Jews against their secular parents.

"There is a polarization going on between religious and secular," says Rabbi Yaakov Frankel, who runs an Orthodox yeshiva in Jerusalem for Jews returning to the faith. "But this must happen before Messiah comes." [4]

Addressing the polarization that had begun within the Jewish community during his time, the legendary Rabbi Samson Raphael Hirsch (1808–1888) declared that God encourages religious Jews to separate themselves from other Jews:

> Gather for Me my devoted ones,
> who uphold My covenant as they
> perform the rite of sacrifice.
>
> —Ps 50:5

"Bound together by their common relationship to God and to His Law," he wrote, "the righteous gather into one united group—lest the desirable elements in the body of God's nation be choked off by less desirable growths." He added, "In the resulting indiscriminate hodge-podge, the entire nation would be lost to the fulfillment of God's aims and purposes."[5]

The kosher and Sabbath and other regulations were meant to force the Israelites to live apart from the contaminating influence of pagans—but since the apostasy of so many Jews after the 1800s Emancipation, those regulations have served to isolate religious Jews from the influence of their less faithful brethren.

Today, the Orthodox descendants of the Pharisees stand out in stark contrast to their non-Orthodox brethren in modern society. And now we are seeing the emergence of the second generation of Jews who turned back to Judaism through the *baal t'shuvah* (master of return) revival that began in the mid-1960s.

4. Cardinale, *The Red Heifer*, 38
5. Hirsch, *The Hirsch Psalms*, 355

~

During one of my visits to Israel with my wife Shirah, we had dinner at the home of Eric Mahr in his home in Neve Yaakov in northern Jerusalem, within sight of two Arab settlements in the West Bank. An old *baal t'shuvah* friend from Buffalo who made aliyah in 1993, Eric discussed the change of heart that must occur among the Jewish people in order to bring Messiah.

"The Talmud says that if the Jews will all be worthy by keeping kosher and Shabbos, God will hurry the Redemption," he said. "If they do not, then every prophecy in the Bible will come true, and there will be 'wars and rumors of wars.'" I smiled to myself to hear my Orthodox friend using an expression coined by Yeshua (Matt 24:6).

Eric added that every major tragedy in Israel has brought people closer to God. Many of them become Orthodox.

Secular Israelis deeply resent the power of the Orthodox, who make up only 20 percent of the country but whose political support is necessary for any government to rule. The Orthodox parties control the education ministry and see to it that yeshiva students, young and old, receive extended military deferments and subsidies to support their families while they spend their days studying the Talmud. (Both Rabbi Hirsch and Maimonides, the legendary codifier of Jewish law, taught that it was wrong to live off charity, jobless, in order to study the Talmud.)

And now Jerusalem is being taken over by the Orthodox and the "ultra-Orthodox"—the Chasidic Jews who dress in the black garb of their eighteenth century ancestors. The presence of the religious is so strong that seculars are moving out of the Holy City. In one recent year, more than 17,000 residents left the city, to be replaced by nearly 11,000 newcomers, most of them Orthodox Jews or Arab citizens of Israel.

True, many ultra-Orthodox still throw stones at vehicles driven by secular Jews on the Sabbath. And their persecution of Jewish believers is shameful. But the Orthodox don't hate secular Jews the way the seculars hate the Orthodox as "religious extremists."

This reminds me of Cain, who must have hated his brother Abel as something of a "fundamentalist" for making himself so pleasing to God.

Secular Jews in Israel are on the run from Judaism and God the Father. For them, Zionism is their state religion. Real religion is given short shrift in the public schools—the homosexual lifestyle is accepted, and the Holocaust is downplayed in the curriculum, lest it overshadow the plight of Palestinian Arabs.

And so, as we watch the hand of the Lord separating the wheat from the chaff, we must be wise. The return of secular Jews to Judaism through the *baal t'shuvah* revival should not be viewed as souls lost to the "slavery of the Law." Rather, religious Jews are repenting, praying and working on their own end-times preparation, and their hearts are turning to obedience to God the Father in the face of bitter recriminations from their own tribe.

Although they were once "hated" for rejecting the New Covenant, the Jews have never lost their election as God's chosen people and are still "loved for the Patriarchs' sake, for God's free gifts are irrevocable." (Rom11:28, David Stern's New Testament)

Yeshua said, "No one can come to Me unless the Father who sent Me draws him." (John 6:44) As a veteran of the charismatic movement that began in the mid-1960s, I believe it was also the Holy Spirit who inspired the *baal t'shuvah* renewal after God gave Jerusalem back to his people in 1967.

When Yochanan the Immerser (John the Baptist) taught the baptism of the Ruach haKodesh, he also said this about the sifting of Israel: "His winnowing fork is in his hand, to clear his threshing floor, and to gather the wheat into his granary, but the chaff he will burn . . ." (Luke 3:17, RSV)

[They] say, "let us possess for ourselves the pastures of God." O my God, make them like whirling dust, like chaff before the wind.

—Ps 83:13–14 (AMP)

Only religious Israelis still believe in the coming of Messiah. They believe that their zeal and obedience will hasten it. When the

Messiah comes, they declare, he will be accepted in the Gentile world, by Muslims and Christians alike. Even Egypt will pay homage to Messiah and be delivered from a plague (finally fulfilling Is 19:21). The question we must ask is: Will these religious Jews be prepared to accept this Messiah when he turns out to be Yeshua of Nazareth?

They will do so only if Jewish believers encourage them in their growing zeal for the coming of Messiah—and remind them that the first believers in Yeshua 2,000 years ago were all Jews who had no intention of leaving Judaism for some new religion. In fact, they had simply joined a new sect of Judaism.

Devout Jews who are offended to hear that they will someday accept Yeshua should be asked this question: Should we believers be offended by your expectation that, when the true Messiah finally comes, Jesus and our religion will be discredited? We are not. If we can still reach out the hand of comfort to you, can't you do the same for us—till Messiah comes and settles his identity once and for all?

We hear almost universal gloom about the gulf that is widening between religious and secular people. But I believe that Yeshua had this polarization in mind when he told the parable of the wheat and the tares (weeds) in a farmer's field.

> ... his enemy came and sowed tares among the wheat ...
> But when the grain had sprouted and produced a crop,
> then the tares also appeared. . .
> The servants said to him,
> "Do you want us then to go and gather them up?"
> But he said, "No, lest while you gather up the tares
> you also uproot the wheat with them."
> —Matt 13:25–29

The Greek word for weeds, *zizanion*, is translated darnel. In his *Rabbinic Commentary on the New Testament*, Samuel Tobias Lachs writes: "Darnel closely resembles wheat, and since it cannot readily be distinguished from wheat, it is left in the field until harvest time. The Rabbis looked upon darnel as a degenerative form of wheat, the produce of sexual excesses that took place in the plant before the Flood. The Rabbis fancifully derive its meaning from *z-n-b*, which means 'to commit fornication.'" [6]

Lachs also finds that verse 29 is reminiscent of "the proverbial saying that together with the thorn the cabbage is smitten." (Baba Qamma 92a).

Yeshua's parable concludes with the farmer telling his servants:

> "Let both grow together until the harvest,
> and at the time of harvest I will say to the reapers,
> 'First gather together tares and bind them in bundles
> to burn them, but gather the wheat into my barn.'"
> —Matt 13:30

How would the servants recognize the mature wheat from the mature tares? Wheat bends in the wind—like believers bowing to the Holy Spirit—but the stubborn tares refuse to bend, standing arrogantly against the wind—making them easy to find and uproot.

This is taking place in our time. Countless American ministers have been exposed and removed from their positions because of their secret sins. This has been accelerating since the scandals of the 1980s when a number of hypocritical televangelists were driven off the air. Scandal has also uprooted rabbis, here and in Israel, after they were found stealing money or abusing children.

> [The righteous] shall be like a tree
> planted by the rivers of water
> that brings forth its fruit in its season,
> whose leaf also shall not wither;
> and whatever he does shall prosper.
> The ungodly are not so,
> but are like the chaff which the wind drives away.
> — Ps 1:34

Sifting is also mentioned in Luke 22:31, where Yeshua rebukes Peter for bragging that he would face prison and death with the Messiah: "Simon, Simon. Indeed, Satan has asked for you, that

6. Lachs, *A Rabbinic Commentary on the New Testament*, 224

he may sift you as wheat." In those days, the harvested grain was thrown into the air by forks so that the wind could carry away the chaff.

Ironically, I believe that the widening polarization across the globe will not only separate faithful Jews and faithful Christians from their unfaithful brethren—but it will also draw these two faithful remnants closer and closer to each other. Dr. Mitch Glaser's Chosen People Ministries sponsored a survey of evangelicals to determine the extent of their present support of Israel. Many churches have joined the BDS (Boycott, Divestment, Sanctions) movement against Israel because of its retaining of Samaria and Judea since recovering them during Six Day War of June 1967.

A whopping 67 percent of evangelicals still have a positive perception of Israel, and only 9 percent feel negative. However, one-quarter of them have "no strong views" about Israel—and for the youngest ones it's an alarming 41 percent. Even more worrisome, younger evangelicals indicated they are more likely to agree that the church has fulfilled or replaced the nation of Israel in God's plan—this, at a time when "replacement theology" has finally been discredited by the church. As for Israel's right to the Holy Land, 70 percent said yes, 6 percent said no, and 25 percent were "unsure."[7]

Faithful Christians and faithful Jews will find themselves in the same boat during the final days. The Holy Spirit will eventually bring God's most faithful Jews—the Orthodox—and his most faithful Christians who worship in Spirit and in truth—closer together, because both groups are fervently intent on preparing for the imminent coming of Messiah, whoever he may be. These are, after all, the final days before the world learns the identity of the Messiah.

～

Whoever the Messiah turns out to be, one side will be vindicated and the other side disappointed. But it need not be quite like that, if the two sides have gone through a gradual merging of interests. The polarization will force us to seek each other as messianic allies

7. Cardinale, "Evangelical Survey on Israel," 9

against a common enemy, our secular persecutors and eventually the Antichrist.

Faithful Jews and Christians will find themselves together on one side of the fence. Jews and Christians persisting in their apostasy will be together on the other. And no one will be permitted to sit on the fence.

I would add that the Holy Spirit brought about the Christian charismatic movement during the same decade that the Jewish *baal t'shuvah* revival began. It is my personal conviction that the Holy Spirit was also behind the latter—and is still working to bring us together, so that the Jews will also be born again in Messiah Yeshua.

God is removing the blinders that he originally put on the Jews so that the Gentiles would also have the opportunity to take part in salvation through the Messiah.

All of this was prophesied by Joel:

> And it shall come to pass afterward
> that I will pour out My Spirit on all flesh;
> your sons and daughters shall prophesy,
> your old men shall dream dreams,
> your young men shall see visions . . .
> And I will show wonders
> in the heavens and on the earth . . .
> before the coming of the great and terrible
> day of the Lord.
> And it shall come to pass
> that whoever calls on the name of the Lord
> shall be saved.
> —Joel 2:28–29

Afterword

THE FOLLOWING ARAB SOURCES on the 1948 exodus of Arabs from western Palestine give irrefutable testimony to the Arab world's full understanding today of how the Arab nations betrayed Palestinian Arabs by encouraging them to flee:

"Mahmoud Abbas (Abu Mazen) wrote an article in March 1976 in *Falastin al-Thawra*, the official journal of the PLO in Beirut: 'The Arab armies entered Palestine to protect the Palestinians from the Zionist tyranny, but instead they abandoned them, forced them to emigrate and to leave their homeland, imposed upon them a political and ideological blockade and threw them into prisons similar to the ghettos in which the Jews used to live in Eastern Europe.'" – *Wall Street Journal*, June,5, 2003.

"The Arab states which had encouraged the Palestine Arabs to leave their homes temporarily in order to be out of the way of the Arab invasion armies, have failed to keep their promise to help these refugees." – Jordan Daily Newspaper *Falastin*, February 19, 1949

"May 15, 1948 arrived; on that very day the Mufti of Jerusalem appealed to the Arabs of Palestine to leave the country because the Arab armies were about to enter and fight in their stead." – Cairo Daily Newspaper *Akhbar El-Yom*, October 12, 1963

"When the Arab delegation entered the conference room, it proudly refused to sign the truce and asked that the evacuation of the Arab population and their transfer to neighbouring Arab countries be facilitated. The Jewish Representatives expressed their profound regret. The Mayor of Haifa adjourned the meeting with a passionate appeal to the Arab population to reconsider its decision…"

—Memorandum by the Arab National Committee to the Arab League Governments on their refusal to sign a truce 27 April 1948[1]

---

1. "Arab Sources on the 1948 Exodus from Israel"

About the Author

ANTHONY CARDINALE IS A Christian Zionist with Jewish bloodlines. This is his fourth book exploring the destiny of Israel and the Jewish people in the coming final days.

A frequent visitor to the Middle East, he was honored by the Society of Professional Journalists for his interviews with Palestinian Arab refugees in Jordan for the *Buffalo News* (and also for the *Jerusalem Post,* which was barred from sending an Israeli reporter into this Arab country). Cardinale disclosed that the land-for-peace proposal, in which Israel would release Gaza and the West Bank for a Palestinian Arab state in return for recognizing Israel, was doomed from the start, because 90 percent of these refugees were from what is now Israel proper and wish to return there.

Cardinale researched his first book, *The Red Heifer: A Jewish Cry for Messiah,* during a residency he was granted in 1998 at Mishkenot Sha'ananim, with its iconic windmill, Jerusalem's guest house for visiting for writers and artists Themes from that book have been expanded in the present book many years later.

During his years with the *Buffalo News,* Cardinale won three dozen journalism awards and was nominated three times for a Pulitzer Prize.

On his first visit to Israel in 1981, he covered the historic World Gathering of Jewish Holocaust Survivors in Jerusalem. Days later, he immersed himself in the Sea of Galilee and dedicated his writing career to the Lord.

With degrees from St. Bonaventure University and Northwestern University, Cardinale has been an adjunct professor at five colleges and is a member of the National Association of Scholars.

He brings to this book his dramatic touch as an award-winning playwright, reproducing scenes and conversations with Jews and Arabs he has met throughout the Middle East.

Bibliography

Abbas, Mahmoud. "The Long Overdue Palestinian State." *New York Times,* May 16, 2011

Afriat, Gil. "October 7 and John 7." *Israel's Restoration,* April 2024, 7

"Ahrar Gaza on Telegram," monitored by MEMRI TV (Middle East Media Research Institute), February 1 and February 21, 2024

"Arab Rejection of '47 Partition Plan Was Error, Palestinian Leader Says." Associated Press, October 28, 2011

"Arab Sources on the 1948 Exodus from Israel." Israel and Judaism Studies, educational website of the New South Wales Jewish Board of Deputies, September 13, 2018

Atbaryan, Galit Distel. "Former Minister and Netanyahu Loyalist Says She Has 'Burning Anger' Against PM." *Times of Israel,* November 16, 2023

Ayalon, Amy, Gilead Sher and Orni Petruschka. "Why Netanyahu Must Go." *Foreign Affairs,* October 31, 2023

Aziz, John. "All My Life, I've Watched Violence Fail the Palestinian Cause." *Atlantic,* November 8, 2023

Baker, Peter. "Inside a U.S. Scramble to Broker a Gaza Deal." *New York Times,* May 8, 2024, A-7

Bard, Mitchell G. *Myths and Facts: A Guide to the Arab-Israel Conflict.* American-Israeli Cooperative Enterprise, 2001, 45

"Ben-Gurion Reiterates Israel Will 'Under No Circumstances' Limit Immigration." Jewish Telegraph Agency, September 21, 1950

Braver, Moshe. "Immigration as a Factor of the Growth of the Arab Village in Eretz-Israel." *Economic Review—Problems of Aliyah and Absorption,* vol. 28, nos. 79, July/September 1975, 20

Burston, Bradley. *The End of Israel: Dispatches from a Path to Catastrophe.* Berkeley: Fryman Press, 2023

Cantor, Elana, email to author, September 20, 2023

Cantor, Ron, "The War over Jewish History," *Tikkun,* January 30, 2023

———. email to author, June 2023

———. email to author, November 2023

Cardinale, Anthony. *The Red Heifer: A Jewish Cry for Messiah*. Baltimore: Lederer, 2012

———. *The Pharisees Are Coming to Jesus: Secret Orthodox Believers in Israel and America*. Maitland, Florida: Xulon, 2021

———. "Encounters in Jordan." *Jerusalem Post*, April 5, 1985, 5

———. "Evangelical Survey on Israel." *Messianic Times*, May/June 2018, 9

———. "Rabbi Kahane's Apartheid Policies." *Liberty: A Magazine of Religious Freedom*. April 1986, 13–15

———. "Rabbi at UB Explains Role of Messiah in Lubavitcher Thinking." *Buffalo News*, February 27, 1993

Cohen, Hillel. *Army of Shadows: Palestinian Cooperation with Zionism, 1917–1948*. Berkeley: University of California Press, 2008

Colon, Peter. "Buying Back Their Land." *Israel My Glory*, September/October 2013, 1

Frantzman, Seth J. "Hamas Is Fueling Fires in Gaza, Lebanon." *International Jerusalem Post*, September 22–28, 2023, 5

———. "How Tensions Between Hamas and Fatah Could Change Gaza." *International Jerusalem Post*, March 22–28, 2024, 12

Greenberg, Rabbi Heschel. "Jewish Unity" lecture at Temple Beth Zion, Buffalo, New York, August 12, 2018

Halperin, David, Israel Policy Forum

Hirsch, Rabbi Samson Raphael. *The Hirsch Psalms*. Jerusalem: Feldheim, 1991, 355

"IDF Elite Intel Officer Warned About Hamas Attacks." *Times of Israel*, November 24, 2023

Ignatius, David. "As Gaza War Enters New Phase, Israel Faces Pressure over Civilian Deaths." Washington Post Writers Group, October 8, 2023

"Israel-Palestinian Hostilities." *New York Times*, May 13, 2021

"Israel Says It Will Keep Land Won in War until Peace Settlement." United Press International Archives, June 27, 1967

Jerusalem Post Staff. "We Have No Right to Throw War in Trash to Save Hostages." *International Jerusalem Post*, May 39, 2024, 4

Kahanov, Rabbi Yoseph. "Confronting Chutzpah with Chutzpah." First Coast Chabad: Jacksonville, Florida, 2006

Kampeas, Ron. "Israeli President Herzog Warns of 'Real Civil War' Amid Battle over Court Reform." *Jewish Telegraph Agency*, March 16, 2023

Karsh, Efraim. "Asaf Romirowsky on Palestine Betrayed." *Jewish Political Studies Review, 22:34 (Fall 2010)*

Keller-Lynn, Carrie. "Lapid: Netanyahu Has 'Lost Control of His Ministers,' Is a Threat to Security." *Times of Israel*, September. 20, 2023

Lachs, Samuel Tobias. *A Rabbinic Commentary on the New Testament: The Gospels of Matthew, Mark and Luke*. Hoboken: Ktav, 1987

Landler, Mark and Ronen Bergman. "As Gaza War Enters New Phase, Israel Faces Pressure over Civilian Deaths." *New York Times*, November 4, 2023

Lazaroff, Tovah. "Female Soldiers Shot in Crotch, Breasts." *International Jerusalem Post,* December 8–14, 2023, 5

Magid, Jacob. "Gallant Warns Israel May Have to Act in Face of 'Intensifying' Threats from Iran." *Times of Israel,* June 1, 2023

Marzouk, Mousa Abu. Arabic TV, November 1, 2023

"Netanyahu in 2012: Democracy Needs 'Strong and Independent' Legal System." *All Israel News* Staff, January 17, 2023

Obeida, Abu. "One Hundredth Day of War." *Palestine Chronicle,* January 14, 2024

Peel Commission Report, July 1937

Peters, Joan. *Since Time Immemorial: The Origins of the Arab-Jewish Conflict over Palestine.* San Francisco: Harper & Row, 1984, 377378

Pipes, Daniel. *International Jerusalem Post,* January 12–19, 2023 Report of UN Special Political Committee, March 11, 2019

Rice, Condoleeza. *No Higher Honor.* New York: Crown, 2011

Rubin, Trudy. "Netanyahu's Attack on Israel's Judiciary." *Philadelphia Inquirer,* March 10, 2023

Shalev, Russell A. "Israel Needs to Talk about the Arab Riots of May 2021." *Fathom,* March 2022

Susser, Leslie. "Democracy Under Threat." *Jerusalem Report,* January 23, 2023, 20

Tarnopolsky, Noga. "Bibi's Rogue Minister Threatens to Plunge Israel into Chaos." *Daily Beast,* January 19, 2023

Times of Israel. "For Most Palestinians, October 7's Savagery Is Literally Unbelievable," November 9, 2024

Twain, Mark. *The Innocents Abroad,* 607

Weinberg, David M. "Enough Truce." *International Jerusalem Post,* November 29, 2023, 20

"Were All the Israelites Deported?" United Church of God, *Beyond Today,* February 16, 2011

Winston, Alex. "A Man on a Mission." *International Jerusalem Post,* March 17, 2004, 18

Zambakari, Christopher. "What Palestinians Really Think of Hamas." *Foreign Affairs,* January 14, 2024

Zimmerman, Michael. "Battir: A Palestinian Village with a Rich, Dramatic Jewish History." *Jerusalem Report,* June 28, 2023, 4

Zohar, Gil. "Media Shocked at Screening of Raw Footage from October 7 Massacre." *Jerusalem Report,* November 27, 2023